Do it

1. Use thin cuts of meat, such as minute steaks, for quickest cooking. Buy tender vegetables, such as snow peas, baby corn, and asparagus, that can be ready in minutes.

2. When possible, buy prepared raw ingredients from salad bars, such as cleaned, trimmed vegetables. In the meat section, buy pretrimmed and ready-to-use cuts such as diced pork or beef for stew, chili, or soup.

3. Keep the food processor out on the countertop and use it to swiftly chop fresh vegetables such as onions and carrots. Immediately after use, rinse the bowl, lid, and blade under hot water and drip dry in the dish drainer.

4. Use stock cubes and hot water instead of chicken stock. Use stock cubes to add more body to stews and sauces. Add one to a pot of rice before cooking for extra flavor.

5. Line baking and roasting pans with aluminum foil so that you don't have to scrub off baked-on food.

One luxurious bubble bath

Access to most comfortable chair and favorite TV show

One half-hour massage (will need to recruit spouse, child, friend)

Time to recline and listen to a favorite CD (or at least one song)

6. When washing dishes by hand. let them drip dry in the drainer. When using the dishwasher. just load them in and don't waste time rinsing first.

7. Make double portions of casseroles and freeze one panful for later use. Make extra rice and pasta to refrigerate and serve later in the week. either reheated in the microwave. or as fried rice or pasta salad.

8. Use a slow cooker that will let stews simmer gently on the counter all day long so you can come home to a finished meal.

9. Make simple desserts from fresh. seasonal fruits such as raspberries. strawberries. or melons in the summer. Serve plain or with brown sugar or whipped cream.

10. Evaluate your strengths when entertaining: Cook the dishes that you're best at or that you're known for. and buy the rest. Serve store-bought foods in your own dishes with a garnish. such as fresh herbs or a sprinkle of spice. that makes it look homemade.

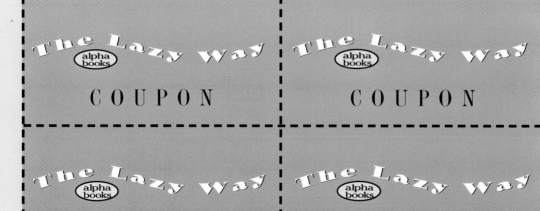

The Lazy Way

alpha books

C O U P O N

The Lazy Way

alpha books

C O U P O N

The Lazy Way

alpha books

C O U P O N

The Lazy Way

alpha books

C O U P O N

cut

Cook
Your
Meals

Cook Your Meals

Sharon Bowers

The Lazy Way™

Macmillan • USA

Macmillan Publishing books may be purchased for business or sales promotional use. For information please write: Special Markets Department, Macmillan Publishing USA, 1633 Broadway, New York, NY 10019.

International Standard Book Number: 0-02-862644-3
Library of Congress Catalog Card Number: 98-87985

01 00 99   8 7 6 5 4 3 2 1

Interpretation of the printing code: the rightmost number of the first series of numbers is the year of the book's printing; the rightmost number of the second series of numbers is the number of the book's printing. For example, a printing code of 99-1 shows that the first printing occurred in 1999.

Printed in the United States of America

Page creation by Carrie Allen, Eric Brinkman, and Heather Pope.

You Don't Have to Feel Guilty Anymore!

IT'S O.K. TO DO IT *THE LAZY WAY!*

It seems every time we turn around, we're given more responsibility, more information to absorb, more places we need to go, and more numbers, dates, and names to remember. Both our bodies and our minds are already on overload. And we know what happens next—cleaning the house, balancing the checkbook, and cooking dinner get put off until "tomorrow" and eventually fall by the wayside.

So let's be frank—we're all starting to feel a bit guilty about the dirty laundry, stacks of ATM slips, and Chinese take-out. Just thinking about tackling those terrible tasks makes you exhausted, right? If only there were an easy, effortless way to get this stuff done! (And done right!)

There is—*The Lazy Way*! By providing the pain-free way to do something—including tons of shortcuts and time-saving tips, as well as lists of all the stuff you'll ever need to get it done efficiently—*The Lazy Way* series cuts through all of the time-wasting thought processes and laborious exercises. You'll discover the secrets of those who have figured out *The Lazy Way*. You'll get things done in half the time it takes the average person—and then you will sit back and smugly consider those poor suckers who haven't discovered *The Lazy Way* yet. With *The Lazy Way*, you'll learn how to put in minimal effort and get maximum results so you can devote your attention and energy to the pleasures in life!

THE LAZY WAY PROMISE

Everyone on *The Lazy Way* staff promises that, if you adopt *The Lazy Way* philosophy, you'll never break a sweat, you'll barely lift a finger, you won't put strain on your brain, and you'll have plenty of time to put up your feet. We guarantee you will find that these activities are no longer hardships, since you're doing them *The Lazy Way*. We also firmly support taking breaks and encourage rewarding yourself (we even offer our suggestions in each book!). With *The Lazy Way*, the only thing you'll be overwhelmed by is all of your newfound free time!

THE LAZY WAY SPECIAL FEATURES

Every book in our series features the following sidebars in the margins, all designed to save you time and aggravation down the road.

- **"Quick n' Painless"**—shortcuts that get the job done fast.
- **"You'll Thank Yourself Later"**—advice that saves time down the road.
- **"A Complete Waste of Time"**—warnings that spare countless headaches and squandered hours.
- **"If You're So Inclined"**—optional tips for moments of inspired added effort.
- **"The Lazy Way"**—rewards to make the task more pleasurable.

If you've either decided to give up altogether or have taken a strong interest in the subject, you'll find information on hiring outside help with "How to Get Someone Else to Do It" as well as further reading recommendations in "If You Want to Learn More, Read These." In addition, there's an only-what-you-need-to-know glossary of terms and product names ("If You Don't Know What It Means/Does, Look Here") as well as "It's Time for Your Reward"—fun and relaxing ways to treat yourself for a job well done.

With *The Lazy Way* series, you'll find that getting the job done has never been so painless!

Series Editor
Amy Gordon

Cover Designer
Michael Freeland

Editorial Director
Gary Krebs

Production Editor
Christina Van Camp

Director of Creative Services
Michele Laseau

What's in This Book

Cook Doesn't Have to Be a 4-Letter Word

Let's get one thing straight. All those superpeople who bake their own bread and sew their own clothes and build their own houses might call us lazy, but what we are is busy. Busy, and tired of spending valuable hours of our lives making food that gets eaten in 15 minutes.

Cooking is the easiest thing to let fall by the wayside when you're busy, because you can get someone to fix your dinner a lot more easily than you can get someone to go to work for you and do your job. But even though buying prepared food or grabbing some takeout relieves you of K.P. duty for one more night, you're losing a lot of control over the quality of your life by not cooking for yourself and ultimately you can start to feel helpless and guilty as you sit down over your TV dinner. But no matter how guilty or miserable you might feel, is it enough to make you want to spend hours in the kitchen each evening?

There is a better way. And it's *The Lazy Way.* Cooking can be faster, better, and even more fun when you learn how to take shortcuts, think simple and fresh, and give yourself permission to take it easy in the kitchen. Making your own food is not only economically sound, but you also know exactly what you're eating. You control the amount of fat, salt, hot pepper sauce, and lemon juice, and you can make your food exactly to your taste; and your family's. What's more, cooking makes a house a home. There are few scents more comforting than that of sizzling garlic or fresh cornbread wafting out from the kitchen around dinnertime.

Whether you're a young single in your first apartment, a busy parent with a full time job, or a grandmother who's spent years putting huge family dinners on the table every Sunday, there's a way to make cooking less of a burden and more of a pleasure. All we need are a few basic ingredients, a hint of know-how (which you already have), and an absolute minimum of initiative. The quick hints and details will let you get the fastest results with the least effort, and start to equalize the discrepancy between how long it takes to prepare a meal, and how long it takes to eat it.

First we'll look at what should be in the pantry, along with ways to organize your kitchen for speed complete with some suggestions for equipment that will help make the workload lighter. Then there are the recipes, for everything from zippy homemade breakfasts to super-quick desserts, all designed so that you can have fresh homemade food as fast as possible.

And all along the way I provide sure-fire shortcuts and tested tips to make your cooking experience even more of a breeze. "Quick n' Painless" offers shortcuts for everything from peeling potatoes to packing lunches. "You'll Thank Yourself Later" has ideas for saving work in the future, such as making a double recipe and freezing half. "A Complete Waste of Time" is made up of three warnings: "The 3 Worst Things to Do..." This way, you'll avoid making mistakes that you'd otherwise spend precious time later trying to fix. "If You're So Inclined," when you have that extra bit of time and energy to gild the lily a bit, provides suggestions for quick sauces and toppings, or imaginative ways to serve what you just cooked. And "The Lazy Way" suggests fun and simple ways to treat and reward yourself, to remind you that cooking isn't all work and no play.

Just imagine. In the newly organized lazy kitchen, designed for the lazy (ahem!) busy person, you can come home from a long day at work, having first stopped off at the gym or picked up the kids at daycare or gone to the store because you've been out of toilet paper for three days (oh right, like that's just me), and throw together a fast, fabulous, hot, homemade meal. And you'll still have the energy left over to pick up your fork and eat it.

And what you'll be eating is real food. The key to the Lazy kitchen is to keep processed foods at a minimum—if you're going to douse a chicken breast with a can of commercially prepared sauce, you might as well have bought the entire dish frozen. And even though the judicious use of prepared foods is necessary from time to time for efficiency, there's a balance in knowing what food to actually cook, and what food to simply apply heat to.

Our emphasis here is on the majority of meals being homemade, with fresh and tasty ingredients, and without all the chemicals and added sugar. If you're jaded from too much sugary canned spaghetti sauce (just read the label—you'll be surprised!), your palate will be in for a shock when you start preparing and eating fresher-tasting food. And if you're a takeout fiend, you'll find that home-cooked food is generally far-less salty than overseasoned restaurant dishes.

But the Lazy kitchen isn't about gourmet cooking. It's about keeping your cabinets reasonably well-stocked while still being flexible, and ready to substitute where necessary. The talent of being able to create dinner where others only see an empty refrigerator isn't an inherent one—it's learned, and you can learn it in minutes. It's just a matter of looking at your pantry differently. I'm a firm believer that if you have pasta or potatoes, you have dinner, even if you eat only noodles with a little garlic sizzled in butter and some Parmesan, or make the potatoes into a thick, creamy soup. Tonight we'll have a starch with a little green salad, and settle down in front of the TV. The dishes can wait.

THE BUSY COOK'S MANIFESTO

I can create dinner out of whatever I find in the kitchen, but I will keep my pantry well-stocked so that I have a good selection of basic ingredients to start with. I will not be a slave to recipes and I will make substitutions whenever I like or wherever necessary. I know how to combine homemade and purchased dishes for a terrific meal. I am not ashamed to openly buy dessert for a dinner party or employ labor-saving devices for simple tasks. If I don't get to the dishes tonight, I'll do them tomorrow.

Part 1

The Painless Pantry

Are You Too Lazy to Read The Painless Pantry?

1 You'd rather leave the carrots and onions out of the recipe than peel and chop them. ☐ yes ☐ no

2 You poach eggs in a 2-gallon stock pot you got as a wedding present 10 years ago. ☐ yes ☐ no

3 The refrigerator contains mustard, an empty pickle jar, and ice. ☐yes ☐ no

Chapter one

Simply Stocked

This is not about organizing yourself and making lots of time-consuming (and always ultimately useless) lists, but about filling your kitchen with the right foods and equipment to ease your way. It's our own happiness and leisure that we busy cooks are concerned about.

The heart of the lazy kitchen is a well-stocked pantry. If you keep basic supplies on hand all the time, you'll be able to pull together a quick and tasty—and healthy—meal, even if you haven't had time to shop the last few days for fresh vegetables and chicken.

The bare necessities for the lazy kitchen are more elaborate than you might think. Make an effort to fill your shelves, fridge, and freezer with lots of dry goods, nonperishables, frozen fish and meat, and fruits and vegetables that keep well. This essentially means making one slightly longer, and a little more expensive than usual, trip to the supermarket to make sure you're well supplied with certain basics, and then shopping (hopefully!) only once a week for perishables such as bread, milk, and fruit.

Warehouses and superstores such as Sam's, Costco, and BJ's are great places to stock up on bulk quantities of nonperishable staples such as olive oil and paper towels. If you have the storage space for the massive quantities you can buy at these stores, you'll save yourself a great deal of shopping time (as well as money). If you don't have access to one of these warehouses (or you don't want to buy a membership card, which can be pricey if you don't plan to use it regularly), buy extras of supplies you use often. You should have more than one can of tomatoes in the cupboard, for example, and an extra jar of mayonnaise still sealed in the pantry for when the one in the fridge runs out.

You can also buy bulk quantities of slightly more extravagant foods, often at lower prices than buying them individually, and further help yourself to make tasty meals with ease. If you have six cans of artichoke hearts in the cupboard, you're more likely to use one in a salad on a regular weeknight than if you only have one—and you're saving it for a special occasion!

Stocking up and buying double (and triple) can add up to huge time savings for the busy cook. Of course, pantries will vary widely, according to individual tastes, but the foods listed as follows are for a wide variety of multiethnic, omnivorous eaters.

The bare necessity ingredients that follow are items to almost always keep on hand. If you have these ingredients, you'll always be able to put together something to eat with ease, even if it's no more elaborate than mac-aroni-and-cheese or a peanut butter-and-jelly sandwich.

First we'll examine what the well-stocked cupboard holds, followed by the refrigerator and freezer. Vegetables and fruits appear at the end as a whole separate category, whether kept in the fridge or out in a hanging basket or vegetable rack, or in a fruit bowl on the counter.

IN THE CUPBOARD AND PANTRY

Bare Necessities

YOU'LL THANK YOURSELF LATER

> Make sure you stock a few boxes of baking soda: one for baking, one for cleaning, one for the fridge to eliminate odors, even one for the freezer to do the same. You don't want to be scooping out of the box in the fridge to add to the cookie dough, nor find yourself without any halfway through a recipe because you finished the box that time you gave the stove a good cleaning.

- Bread (a loaf of bakery sourdough and a loaf of moist, bran-filled brown at my house; you may only eat one or the other, but consider also keeping some sandwich rolls or buns on hand for casual suppers)

- Coffee and/or tea (you may prefer to store your coffee in the freezer to keep it fresh longer)

- Flour (unbleached all-purpose for general cooking, but also possibly a stoneground whole wheat for breads)

- Sugar (brown and white)

- Baking soda

- Baking powder

- Cornstarch

- Rice (plain white is always useful; brown has lots of extra fiber and vitamins, but remember that it takes much longer to cook)

QUICK 🔲 PAINLESS

Any chef worth his or her toque would rather die than not make and use homemade stock for soups and sauces. But for my lazy kitchen, stock cubes are the way to go. I keep beef, chicken, and vegetable flavors on hand, and I use a top-quality brand that never lets me down. If you have lots of kitchen energy, by all means make homemade stock and freeze it in an ice-cube tray. But most busy cooks can find better things to do with their time.

- Pasta (a long thin type such as spaghetti or fettuccine; a short type such as shells or rotini; and a package of super-quick cooking angel hair, also called capellini, for very busy nights)
- Olive oil (extra virgin for all dressings and sauces and to drizzle over salads or brush on bruschetta or roasted vegetables; you may want to keep some cheaper, less virgin oil on hand for general cooking)
- Cooking oil (canola, corn, or other poly- or monounsaturated oil; I prefer olive oil for nearly everything, but sometimes you need a completely flavorless oil like one of these, for stir-frying or quick breads)
- Vinegar (red wine vinegar for most cooking and sauces; white or cider vinegar for cooking and domestic uses such as cleaning the coffee maker)
- Canned tomatoes (whole and crushed)
- Canned beans (black, kidney, cannellini, pinto)
- Spices (cinnamon, chili powder, cumin, curry powder, nutmeg)
- Dried herbs (basil, oregano, rosemary, thyme)
- Soy sauce
- Worcestershire sauce
- Tuna (the chunk light kind packed in water is best for sandwiches; the more expensive white albacore type makes a luxurious salad)
- Peanut butter
- Stock cubes (beef, chicken, vegetable)
- Breakfast cereal

Useful Extras

- Rolled oats (not only for breakfast but for adding to quick breads and making toppings for fruit crisps)

- Cocoa

- Honey

- Raisins

- Chocolate chips

- Nuts, chopped or whole (almonds, walnuts, peanuts, pecans)

- Tomato paste

- Canned soups (at least one can of cream of mushroom and/or cream of celery for a quick tuna casserole)

- Canned vegetables (such as good quality peas, green beans, corn; not to be relied on as your main source of vegetables but there for the occasional casserole or side dish)

- Sun-dried tomatoes (the oil-packed ones save time hydrating, but can add an oily flavor to some dishes; it's not impossible to find soft ones packed in a canister without oil.)

- Canned broth (for most cooking purposes, a stock cube is fine for the busy cook; but a good quality, low-sodium chicken broth makes a fine base for a quick soup and beef broth becomes an elegant last-minute consommé when you lace it with sherry)

- Powdered milk

QUICK 🖤 PAINLESS

Buying honey that comes in a squeeze bottle saves time scooping and cleaning sticky drips. If your preferred brand is sold in a jar, pour the honey into a clean squeeze bottle, like those yellow mustard containers. (Just make sure you label it as "honey" before anyone makes a honey hot dog.)

- UHT Milk (for emergency use in your morning coffee)
- Instant mashed potatoes (absolutely not to be eaten as mashed potatoes but really good for topping shepherd's pie and thickening soups in a pinch)
- Hot sauce
- Cornmeal
- Spices (allspice, cardamom, cinnamon sticks, cloves, coriander, pumpkin pie spice, star anise)
- Dried herbs (sage, tarragon, marjoram, lemon thyme)
- Molasses (for gingerbread)
- Vanilla (real vanilla essence, not synthetic, for the best flavor in your quick baked goods)
- Popcorn (either regular kernels or microwave)

Treat Yourself

- Packaged cookies
- Cake mix
- Container of cake frosting
- Brownie mix
- Dried mushrooms (such as shiitake or porcini)
- Sesame oil
- Canned garbanzo beans (great for hummus and salads)
- Chinese noodles

QUICK n' PAINLESS

Many housewares stores, kitchen specialty shops, and cookware mail order catalogs offer spice caddies that not only house spices in one neat unit, but often include the spices themselves. You can even go "gourmet" and buy dispensers for whole spices. Here the seeds (such as whole cumin) are housed in individual units, each of which is equipped with its own grinder. Fresh and fancy!

- Basmati rice
- Arborio rice
- Canned good-quality chili
- Commercial spaghetti sauce (look for one without added sugar for the best flavor)
- Canned chipotles in adobo
- Canned sardines
- Anchovy paste (for Caesar salad dressing)
- Coconut milk
- Marshmallows
- Spices (saffron, garam masala, Chinese 5-spice powder)
- Pine nuts (much cheaper to buy in bulk from a gourmet store than to buy a tiny little pre-packaged can or jar)

IN THE REFRIGERATOR

This is the first place you look to see if there's anything to eat in the house, and it's dismaying to find little besides mustard and a withered carrot, so keep your fridge well-but-vigilantly stocked. In my experience, foods in the refrigerator always keep fresh a little longer than experts say they will. Common sense will tell you when a refrigerated food is past its prime, but items such as marmalade, pickles, and even yogurt, can last much longer than we like to even think about! Even so, if you're not going through your bare necessities at the

IF YOU'RE SO INCLINED

If you are a real fan of Asian cooking, you might want to purchase both types of sesame oil: the light kind (lighter in both color and flavor), which is great for everything from salad dressings to sautéing, and the dark toasted sesame oil which has a much stronger flavor and fragrance. Toasted sesame oil is not for cooking, but is usually used to accent a dish—drizzled on top or stirred in at the last minute. (It's also terrific in tuna salad!

Don't forget to pick up some fresh herbs, available in small packs in the produce section, on your weekly shopping trip for perishables. They add real zest and savor to salads, vegetables, and meat dishes, and cannot be replaced by dried herbs. There's a drastic difference between the effects and tastes of dried and fresh, and it varies from herb to herb. Dried oregano is a pungent addition to spaghetti sauce, while fresh adds a far more delicate flavor. Fresh parsley has an almost peppery green taste, while dried parsley tastes like shredded paper.

rate you expect, cut back on buying, and toss out all the old stuff periodically.

Bare Necessities

- Milk
- Eggs
- Butter or margarine
- Cheese (at least Cheddar and Parmesan)
- Mayonnaise
- Mustard (Dijon and yellow or spicy brown)
- Ketchup
- Grape or strawberry jelly (for peanut butter-and-jelly sandwiches, of course)

Useful Extras

- Orange (or other fruit) juice
- Soda or sparkling water
- Buttermilk (I like to have buttermilk on hand for quick breads and biscuits, but it may not have any part in your kitchen repertoire. It will keep for a long time if you do buy it; if you don't, you can substitute plain yogurt for any recipe that calls for buttermilk.)
- Cottage or ricotta cheese
- Sour cream
- Plain yogurt
- Salsa

Treat Yourself

- Fresh herbs (basil, cilantro, rosemary, sage, flat-leaf parsley)

- Fresh pasta (don't bother with fresh spaghetti or fettuccine, but fresh ravioli or tortellini is a treat)

- Chicken broth in resealable boxes (this recent introduction to the market means fresher, tastier chicken broth to splash into quick sauces or soups, rather than using stock cubes or canned)

- Cream (the high fat content means it can keep for weeks, and even just a splash in a sauce or soup makes a real difference in flavor and texture)

- Pickled jalapeños (for making homemade salsa)

- Olives (not canned or bottled but real cured olives from a deli or gourmet shop, either green or black)

- Pesto

- Chutney (if you cook or eat much Indian food, a fruit chutney such as pear or mango is an indispensable condiment for a plate of hot curry; but chutney is also great on cheese and meat sandwiches)

- Miso paste (for super-quick miso soup)

- Tahini (the sesame paste necessary for hummus, it will keep for a very long time; if in doubt, sniff to see if you detect a rancid smell)

A COMPLETE WASTE OF TIME

The 3 Worst Things to Do with Fresh Herbs:

1. Substituting the same amount of dried herb in a recipe calling for fresh.

2. Using too much and too many types of fresh herbs in one dish, thereby making the flavors fight each other.

3. Letting them sit in the refrigerator until they've dried out and are flavorless.

IN THE FREEZER

In general, I prefer to keep and prepare food that is as fresh as possible, instead of making an entire meal directly from the freezer. But there's no denying that a well-stocked freezer is an absolute requirement for the busy kitchen. You can keep meat frozen and thaw it in the microwave for a quick dinner (or take it out in the morning to thaw on the counter). Fish fillets can go in the oven or the sauté pan with ice crystals still clinging to them. The freezer holds emergency bread for those mornings when you're out of fresh bread—two frozen slices into the toaster and you're ready for breakfast.

Bare Necessities

- Ice
- Bread
- Fish fillets
- Chicken breasts
- Hamburger (in 1- or ½-pound packs)
- Steak or pork chops (same number of chops as family members per pack)
- Peas
- Corn
- Spinach

Useful Extras

- Frozen pancakes and waffles
- Shrimp (for fried rice)
- Lima beans or other frozen vegetables (frozen limas are far better than canned or dried)

A COMPLETE WASTE OF TIME

The 3 Worst Things to Do with Frozen Food:

1. Cook all your meals with foods taken from the freezer.

2. Allow food to become stale and freezer-burned by not sealing it well.

3. Thaw and refreeze food before cooking.

- Bread dough (available ready-made in the freezer section; perfect for fast, almost-homemade loaves and sweet rolls)
- Pita bread
- Tortillas (flour and corn)

Treat Yourself

- Crab claws
- Ravioli (buy fresh and freeze, or buy frozen)
- Ice cream
- Cake layers (unfrosted layers made and frozen by you, or a good quality baked and frosted cake for those times you forget a birthday)
- Danish pastry (for a leisurely Saturday morning)
- Raspberries

IN THE VEGETABLE BASKET

You should keep these long-storing vegetables on hand (these lists do not include seasonal vegetables such as corn-on-the-cob, fresh tomatoes, summer squash, fresh spinach, asparagus, varieties of lettuce, etc.). The following vegetables are available year-round; as long as you have them, you'll always have something to eat in the house. Most of these do not have to be stored in the refrigerator (unless noted), but can be kept on the counter, in hanging baskets, in a vegetable drawer, or in a plastic vegetable rack (the ones on wheels are very handy).

YOU'LL THANK YOURSELF LATER

If you have to bake a birthday cake, use a packaged cake mix (of course!); and while you're at it, bake two. The extra layers (or one 9" × 13" rectangle) store very well if they're cooled, removed from the pan, and wrapped tightly in plastic wrap and placed in the freezer. Then you'll have a cake ready to pull out and frost (with ready-made or homemade frosting) for school bake sales, dinner parties, or a birthday that creeps up on you.

Buy interesting or regionally made condiments to top simply cooked chicken and fish. If you look around in the condiment section, you may be surprised to find that often the most generic supermarket will carry one or two cottage-industry sauces and toppings, from unusually flavored mustards to relishes to homemade barbecue or hot chili sauce. Gourmet markets will usually have a selection from around the world.

Bare Necessities

- Potatoes
- Onions
- Garlic
- Lettuce (in the fridge and not iceberg; say hello to romaine, Bibb, mesclun, or red for a change)
- Cucumber (in the fridge)
- Carrots (in the fridge)

Useful Extras

- Celery (in the fridge; even when it's limp, it's usable for cooking)
- Peppers (refrigerate; green and/or red)
- Ginger
- Sweet potatoes
- Cabbage (can go in the refrigerator, especially after it's been cut)

Treat Yourself

- Celeriac (also called celery root; like a big brown turnip, combined with a mild nutty celery. Great when boiled and mashed into potatoes or shredded for salads.)
- Jerusalem artichokes (a nutty tuber with a mildly artichoke-like flavor)

- Artichokes (can go in fridge)
- Cardoons (these artichoke flavored stalks are very popular in Italy and are showing up more and more in U.S. markets)

IN THE FRUIT BOWL

The minimal fruit bowl should contain the following Bare Necessity fruits that stay fresh and edible for many days, even weeks. Softer fruits, listed under Useful Extras, require a little more attention and can't be expected to stay fresh for weeks. Last are pricier seasonal fruits, listed under Treat Yourself, which should be stored in the refrigerator and preferably eaten the same day.

Bare Necessities

- Apples
- Oranges
- Grapefruit
- Lemons (keep longer in the fridge)

Useful Extras

- Bananas
- Kiwi fruit
- Grapes
- Pears

IF YOU'RE SO
INCLINED

With increasing evidence that agri-chemicals are detrimental to our health, you may want to buy organic foods. They're becoming more widely available, and the difference in flavor between an organically grown orange and a mass-produced one is astonishing. Some large cities even have delivery services that bring organic fruits and vegetables to your house once a week.

The only list that the busy cook keeps is one for shopping. Attach a magnet-backed notepad and a pencil on a string to the front of your refrigerator, and keep a running grocery list. Whenever you use up an ingredient from your well-stocked pantry, from milk to pine nuts, make a note of it. (Don't assume that you'll simply remember the basics such as bread.) Rip off the top page each time you go to the grocery store, and you'll ensure that your pantry stays fully stocked.

Treat Yourself

- Raspberries
- Strawberries
- Blackberries
- Blueberries

Keeping the pantry stocked should be the most work the busy cook has to do in the kitchen. If you put in the little bit of effort to keep your cupboards and fridge full, then you'll neither be wracking your brain as you stare into empty shelves, nor will you have to work up a sweat to put together a fast and flavorful meal.

Getting Time on Your Side

	The Old Way	The Lazy Way
Staring into refrigerator trying to figure out what to make for dinner	15 minutes	$1^1/_2$ minutes
Making a list for weekly shopping trip for perishables and stocking up	20 minutes (just before leaving)	2 seconds (when you run out of something)
Putting together a romantic birthday dinner for someone special	3 hours	30 minutes (you've got fresh pasta and frozen cake layers in the freezer!)
Making stock	2 hours	3 minutes (with stock cube)
Making mashed potato topping for shepherd's pie	1 hour	5 minutes
Length of time a container of plain yogurt will stay usable in the fridge	1 week	4 weeks

Chapter
two

The Epicure's Exertion-Free Equipment

Once you have your pantry groaning with supplies, you're nearly ready to cook. First, though, you can use certain equipment to make things easier. Plenty of books tell you that you can get by with the bare minimum of a large and small kitchen knife, and a cutting board—and that may be true—but it's not the lazy way.

I'm not suggesting that you need an appliance to do every task, but I can't get by without certain tried-and-true multi-purpose items, such as a food processor. A good rule of thumb is to avoid any appliance that is only designed to accomplish one task (with a few obvious exceptions, such as coffee makers). A novelty appliance (for example, one that heats only hot dogs, shapes and fries only hamburgers, or makes only yogurt) is usually an appliance that gets a few test runs and then sits on the shelf collecting dust.

Even though I'm not crazy about appliances with limited uses, I do have space in my kitchen for a few gadgets that make life simpler. Chief among them are my garlic toys, including a garlic peeler, a garlic press, and a garlic mandolin. The peeler is a particularly nifty item—it's a rubber tube in which you insert cloves of garlic. A firm roll back and forth on the counter and naked cloves drop out. (You can also use it for shallots.) The press quickly minces 1 or 2 cloves, and the mandolin, a flat metal blade with a plastic carriage to hold the garlic, will shred or slice large quantities of garlic in record time.

When it comes to electrical appliances, though, what we busy cooks need are items such as food processors, hand blenders, beaters, and microwaves, which actually save work and can be cleaned quickly and easily. We also need a basic stock of pots, pans, bowls, dishes, and utensils that are helpful and multipurpose.

APPLIANCES

Don't go to an upmarket, specialty store to buy your kitchen appliances. Most of them can be purchased far more reasonably at one of those warehouse-like home and garden stores, or at any of the national chain discount stores. You can usually find the same brand names as those you find at any specialty store.

When it comes to brand-name appliances, it doesn't always make much difference whether you buy the top-of-the-line or the lower-priced version. The exception is for machines that need powerful motors to drive them, such as food processors and standing mixers. You need a motor that won't burn out if you whizz it for five minutes to grind almonds or knead bread dough. The engine

IF YOU'RE SO
INCLINED

Depending on the tastes of your household members, you may want a few appliances that do only one thing (and even if you don't need them, you'll get them as gifts). My number one choice is a waffle maker. Mine may sit and gather dust on a shelf most of the year, but it earns its keep when I make waffles on Christmas morning.

size and strength is less important when it comes to electric beaters and hand blenders, which are usually only used for lighter, more liquid tasks, such as beating egg whites and pureeing soups.

Bare Necessities

Food processor: The end-all and be-all of the lazy kitchen. It chops everything from vegetables to bread crumbs to meat, mixes batters and doughs, makes sauces, and so on. Buy the best-quality food processor you can afford, preferably by a recognized maker. In this case, you'll really get what you pay for in terms of the power of the motor (so it doesn't burn out on big jobs like bread dough), sharpness and durability of blades, and versatility when it comes to attachments.

Hand blender: A very quick and handy way to puree soups directly in the pot, or smooth sauces that get curdled or lumpy.

Microwave: For cooking vegetables, making superquick scrambled eggs and bacon, melting butter or shortening, or reheating and thawing frozen food.

Slow cooker: Allows long, slow, unattended cooking of stews; perfect for cooking dried beans (and you don't have to soak them first when using one of these) and tenderizing tough cuts of meat.

Useful Extras

Mini prep food processor: It's not an absolute necessity the way a big food processor is, but these mini processors, which hold about 1 cup of ingredients, are terrific for very quickly chopping an onion, a couple of cloves of

Electric beaters may sound redundant if you already have a food processor and hand blender, but it's worth it to have this reasonably priced piece of equipment. After seeing prices that ranged up to $40.00 for a top brand name, I bought my hand beaters for $8.99 at a large household store. I use them frequently for quickly mixing cakes or batters, beating egg whites or cream, and whipping up fluffy mashed potatoes. The only items you have to wash are the two beaters, and they can go in the dishwasher.

garlic, some ginger, or a few fresh herbs, not to mention quickly blending salad dressings or small quantities of sauces.

Blender: Although food processors perform most of the actions of a blender, I still frequently use my blender to make fruit and yogurt drinks; pancake, waffle, and crepe batter; sauces and dressings, etc.

Standing mixer: You need one with a motor strong enough to make bread, if you're so inclined. For mixing cakes or batter, standing mixers are great because they keep mixing while you use your hands to gather and add ingredients.

Electric can opener with knife sharpener: Strictly a matter of what you're used to. In terms of the time it takes to open a can, it's about the same whether you use an electric or handheld opener. But a good electric one lets you attach a can and walk away, and the knife sharpener is a nice detail.

Toaster oven: Not only makes toast but melts cheese onto toast or over a sandwich (such as a tuna melt); reheats pizza, makes croutons and bruschetta.

Treat Yourself

Dishwasher: Some people think this is a bare necessity, but I lived in NY without one for years and lived to tell the tale.

Electric carving knife: For big jobs such as holiday turkey, ham, or roast beef.

Outdoor gas grill: Unlike charcoal, gas makes grilling quick and easy. When it comes to sizzling steaks over a high heat, gas grills can be not only fun, but practical.

Electric kettle: These gadgets are ubiquitous in the U.K., where a quick cup of tea is considered a bare necessity, but they're more of a luxury for the U.S. kitchen. You fill the kettle and click it on, and it then boils in mere minutes and clicks off.

Instant boiling water kitchen tap: Can be fitted to your regular kitchen tap—you have instant boiling water, whether for a cup of instant coffee or a potful of pasta.

GADGETS AND MISCELLANEOUS EQUIPMENT

Bare Necessities

Large and small mixing bowls: Either one of each or a graduated set. Make sure that your large bowl is big enough to toss a pasta, lettuce, or potato salad; and that your small bowl is big enough to hold a couple of eggs for beating.

Measuring cups for dry ingredients: A set of stainless steel measuring cups in 1 cup, ½ cup, ⅓ cup, and ¼ cup sizes. Having cups in any additional sizes will just add extra clutter.

1- and 2-cup Pyrex measuring cups for liquids: You could make do with a 1-cup liquid measure, but in addition to measuring all liquids, you'll reach for this handy size glass container to quickly beat an egg or two, or mix up salad dressing.

Measuring spoons: Preferably stainless steel as plastic measures can start to feel greasy with extensive use. Buy the kind that's linked with a ring, like a set of keys, so they're easily found.

YOU'LL THANK YOURSELF LATER

If you're in the market for a new set of mixing bowls, consider buying sets that come with lids. This way, you don't have to transfer left-overs into separate closed containers and will have one less dish to wash.

QUICK n PAINLESS

Pepper mill: Freshly ground pepper is a quality-of-life issue, so get one that's sturdy and functional.

Salad spinner: Salad leaves must be washed and must be dried; a salad spinner offers the quickest, most efficient way to accomplish both jobs. Fill the outer bowl with cold water to freshen and clean lettuce leaves, then lift them from the water into the inner basket, letting the dirt sink to the bottom. Dump the dirty water and spin.

Cutting board for meat: To be used only for meat, poultry, and fish. After years of saying that plastic boards were safer and more resistant to bacteria than wood, scientists have reversed themselves. The same minute cuts that hold bacteria in the wood also appear in the plastic, so choose whatever style of cutting board you like. Just be sure to wash it with soap and water.

Cutting board for all other foods: For sanitary reasons, don't let meat touch this one, and vice versa.

Colander: If you have a stainless steel one, it can double as a steamer basket when set atop a pan of boiling water. Plastic is perfectly acceptable, but make sure your colander is big enough to drain a whole pot of pasta.

Useful Extras

Magnetic knife rack: Position it on the wall right above your cutting board to keep knives close at hand. Blades stay sharper than they do when stored in a knife block.

Pastry brush: For brushing olive oil on meat, fish, or bruschetta; brushing barbecue sauce on grilled chicken, etc.

Treat Yourself

Parmesan grater: So you can always grate fresh Parmesan over your pasta, right at the table.

Garlic peeler: A rubber tube about 6 inches long and 1½ inches in diameter. When you drop in a few cloves of garlic and firmly roll under your flattened palm, it whips the paper off garlic and shallots. Available in any housewares store, these gadgets work so well and so impressively that you may end up peeling every clove of garlic in the house when you first bring it home.

Pizza cutter: If you buy a good quality, sharp-edged pizza wheel, these tools are the fastest way to cut up a pizza. If you're not going to use one very often, use your kitchen shears (rinsing immediately after use). Store pizza cutters somewhere other than your utensil drawer, so you don't inadvertently cut your hand when rifling for other tools.

POTS AND PANS

Many cooks continue using the same pots and pans that they inherited from their mothers, or those that were received as wedding gifts many years ago. My mother used her wedding pots for 25 years, until she suddenly realized that she was entitled to buy exactly what she wanted and have a set that suited her cooking needs. The busy cook needs to come to that same conclusion.

Good pots and pans mean you don't have to think about them. They should do the job quickly and efficiently, and not require a whole lot of clean-up, which is

YOU'LL THANK YOURSELF LATER

Keep a small dish brush near the sink and brush your box grater clean if you've grated something relatively dry, such as nutmeg or lemon zest. If you've grated something stickier, such as cheese, use the brush and hot soapy water to clean it in a snap—much easier than rubbing it with a cloth.

why I prefer nonstick whenever possible. It's the difference between soaking a stainless steel skillet with the remains of scrambled egg all day long, and then scrubbing it out with a messy steel wool pad covered in egg bits, or taking a paper towel and wiping out the streak of egg left on the nonstick surface. I like pans to not be encrusted with food after I use them, and that includes roasting pans. Wax paper and aluminum foil were made for the busy cook and I make a point of using them.

Although copper pots look beautiful in magazine photos, they're not necessarily practical; if you don't keep them shiny, they lose the heat-distributing qualities you bought them for. Heat-proof glass saucepans look interesting but are not ideal for cooking because they distribute heat unevenly. For the lazy kitchen, a good solid set of heavy-bottomed stainless steel is ideal. Even more important are your nonstick pans. Get the best ones you can afford, and treat them right, never using metal utensils. When the nonstick surface eventually wears away, and it will with almost all brands, replace that skillet or pot with a new nonstick one.

Bare Necessities

Stainless steel saucepans: At least three sizes, with matching lids.

Nonstick sauté or omelet pan: Big enough to hold a couple of chicken breasts or make a 4- to 6-egg omelet. (Do not buy a thin, light, or cheap pan—these wear out in weeks. Get a heavy pan with a tough nonstick coating made by a recognized manufacturer.)

If you're in the market for new pots, avoid buying the "glass" kind, which distribute heat poorly. But you may want to consider buying those with heatproof glass lids. That way, you can see when the water is boiling or if the rice is bubbling too much.

Stoneware or glass casserole and baking dishes: White Pyrex looks good, but you can't scrub it with steel wool or any other metal scrubber or it will be covered in black marks. Get sturdy, easily cleaned, dishwasher-safe baking dishes, and if you buy white Pyrex dishes, scrub them with plastic pads or scrubbers.

Useful Extras

Large nonstick skillet: If you're cooking for more than two, you need a nonstick skillet that's big enough to hold dinner for everyone. Again, get a heavy pan with a good tough coating.

Small nonstick saucepan: For heating milk and making sauces.

Stove-top grill pan: Often made of cast iron and capable of being heated to a very high temperature, the ridges on the bottom of these indoor grilling pans simulate the grill marks that you get when cooking on an outdoor gas or charcoal grill. It's the only way to simulate the grill effect.

Muffin tin: To be used with muffin paper liners.

Loaf pan: In addition to baking the frozen bread dough in your freezer, you can use it for meat loaf and quick breads.

Baking sheet: A regular flat cookie sheet, with a rim on only one side, is best for everyday use.

Roasting pan and rack: Make sure the sides aren't too high, or you won't brown the food inside that well. Low-sided roasters cook faster by letting the heat reach the food more evenly.

A COMPLETE WASTE OF TIME

The 3 Worst Things to Do with Nonstick Pans:

1. Heat them without anything in them.

2. Use any utensils other than wood or plastic on them.

3. Clean them with a metal scrubber.

Treat Yourself

Wok: Stir frying is quicker and easier in a wok, but you can also use a large nonstick skillet.

Steamer basket: To preserve color and vitamins in quick-cooking vegetables.

Insulated baking sheet: Keeps cookies and rolls from burning; but not so good for roasting vegetables.

UTENSILS

Most utensil drawers are a mishmash of pieces we've collected over the years, but shove aside the corn holders, fish forks, and swizzle sticks and take a good look at your basic equipment. Clear out all the gadgets you haven't used in years and make sure you have a full set of basic tools such as stirring spoons, slotted spoons, spatulas, tongs, etc., including plastic tools for your nonstick pans and metal tongs and spatulas for the outdoor grill or grill pan, where the heat is too high to use plastic.

Knives in particular should be the best quality you can afford. You've heard it before, but let me confirm again that a sharp knife is safest because it requires less pressure.

Bare Necessities

Large chef knife: A high-carbon steel that holds a sharp edge. Keep it sharp and on a knife rack so it doesn't joggle against other utensils in the drawer nor cut your hand when you're reaching in.

Paring knife: For cutting apples, potatoes, or one clove of garlic. The blade should be small, sharp, and agile.

QUICK n' PAINLESS

Instead of trying to chop fresh herbs with a knife, where the small leaves tend to spread and stick onto the cutting board, simply hold the herbs over the bowl or pot and cut the greens with kitchen shears, allowing the snipped herbs to fall directly into the dish.

Serrated bread knife: Terrific for more than just bread; cuts tomatoes, onions, cucumbers, and soft fruit cleanly.

Scissors: Again, buy the strongest, best-quality kitchen shears you can find; and be sure they're dishwasher-safe. Use them for as many tasks as you can instead of knives—it's faster.

Wooden or plastic spoons: To use with nonstick pans.

Vegetable peeler: Much faster than a paring knife for peeling potatoes, apples, carrots, etc.

Slotted spoon: For lifting cooked vegetables or poached eggs, etc. out of the cooking liquid.

Spatula: for turning meat, lifting fried eggs out of the pan, taking cookies off the baking sheet, etc.

Rubber scraper: To get the last bit out of the bowl.

Small balloon whisk: For quickly beating eggs or vinaigrette.

Ladle: For serving soups and stews.

Bottletop/can opener: For pouring, get the kind with a triangular tip at one end to notch cans, such as tomato juice and evaporated milk. Ideally, buy a magnetic one that can stick to the front of the fridge.

Useful Extras

Garlic press: With a cleaner attached.

Extra-large serving spoon: Preferably heat-resistant plastic, for serving out of your nonstick as well as other pans.

Extra-large balloon whisk: Certain electric mixing tools have made large whisks obsolete for whipping cream or

YOU'LL THANK YOURSELF LATER

Buy a vegetable peeler with a rubber handle. Not only will you have a better grip when peeling vegetables (which means the peeling goes a lot quicker), but you will also be able to create carrot and zucchini ribbons. They may sound fancy, but they're simply thin strips. Shave the carrot ribbons directly into a salad; zucchini ribbons can be quickly sautéed in garlic and olive oil for a delicious side dish.

egg whites, but they're still useful to have on hand for quick jobs such as beating a bowlful of eggs for scrambled eggs or giving a quick whisk to a lumpy sauce.

Cantilever corkscrew: The kind with arms that requires no extra effort from you.

Potato masher: Beaters make fluffy mashed potatoes; hand-held mashers make fast ones.

Treat Yourself

Pasta server: Surprisingly efficient and useful, these wooden or plastic tools feature teeth to grab the slippery cooked pasta (though you can also make do by lifting spaghetti out with a fork and spoon).

Small grater for nutmeg and citrus zest: Like fresh pepper, fresh nutmeg and citrus zest bring foods alive with flavor.

Poultry shears: The fastest, easiest way to cut up a chicken.

Meat cleaver: A small one is useful for more than meat—if you're adept with one of these, it's the only chopping knife you need.

Chopsticks: For eating Chinese food, of course, but a pair also works well for beating eggs and for stirring beaten eggs into fried rice.

Chinese soup spoons: The large flat-bottomed kind. Not only good for eating soup, but also for tasting dishes while you cook.

The equipment and supplies described here would make for a particularly well stocked kitchen, but don't assemble them all in haste. As you start cooking dinner more often using the lazy method, see how you cook and what you really need. The best rule for kitchen equipment and utensils is "use it or lose it." I can't live without my garlic press, but if you find that you prefer to mince with a knife or a mini food processor, pass your press along to a friend or a charity so that it isn't cluttering your drawer when you're trying to find the tools you really need.

Now that you've got your lazy kitchen fully equipped, break out the blender and treat yourself to an ice cold margarita. Olé!

The Lazy Way

Getting Time on Your Side

	The Old Way (by hand)	The Lazy Way (with appliance)
Finely chopping head of cabbage	15 minutes	3 minutes
Whipping cream	8 minutes	2 minutes
Peeling and cutting garlic	4 minutes	1 minute
Beating egg whites stiff	10 minutes	2 minutes
Pureeing soup	10 minutes	1 minute
Mixing and kneading bread dough	20 minutes	5 minutes

Part 2

The Gourmet Express: Tips

Are You Too Lazy to Read The Gourmet Express?

1 You have to look behind the bleach to find the oregano. ☐ yes ☐ no

2 You only use the blender to mix daiquiris. ☐ yes ☐ no

3 You'd rather break a plate than wash it. ☐ yes ☐ no

Easy Reach: Organizing the Speedy Kitchen

The ideal lazy kitchen is attractive but not necessarily pretty. There's no room in this workspace for excessive bric-a-brac, such as crocheted jar tops and painted trivets that can't hold hot pans. Without redesigning and making a huge project out of the job, a little rearranging allows you to reorganize your kitchen in one fell swoop to make it work better for you.

Look at where you stand to work. Is the path clear throughout your kitchen triangle—sink to cooktop to refrigerator—or do you have to go around the table to get to the fridge? Do you have to lift cups and bowls to take out dinner plates? Are you constantly shoving packages and sacks around in the cabinets to find that one last can of tomatoes you're sure is in there?

Kitchen decor should be utilitarian, first and foremost. The counter should boast a food processor, a microwave, a bowl of fruit, and an olive oil can instead of a flower vase and a

Even if you're not ready to throw away, give away, or donate to charity all the excessive or unused utensils and equipment in your kitchen, take it out of the kitchen for now, anyway. Pack it all in a box and put it under a bed, in the garage, or on a high shelf. If you really do need that melon-baller, return it to the utensil drawer. But if you haven't used it after a year, you'll probably never miss it. Meanwhile, you'll have spent a year working in an accessible, easy-to-use, clutter-free kitchen.

framed picture. It's primarily a working room, and you should think of it like a workshop. You can decorate with attractive versions of useful objects, such as a pretty fruit bowl, an interesting oil can, and color coordinated appliances.

If your kitchen and dining room are the same room, save the space around the table for photos, flowers, or wall hangings, instead of putting them around your countertop or work space. If the kitchen is so small that you're lucky to squeeze a table in, it's all the more important that you don't clutter up your scant workspace with anything besides tools for the job at hand.

Real kitchens, kitchens that are used, do not have spotless, empty countertops and sparkling stoves. You want to be comfortable, of course, and you can do that with bright colors on the walls and good lighting. But you want to make sure that your most important equipment and supplies are where you can lay hands on them with ease. Take a few minutes to shift things around. If you're constantly reaching over one item to get to another (and we all know who we are—it just becomes a habit!), move the espresso pot to the back or into a closet, and put the coffee filters out front.

ORGANIZING CUPBOARDS AND CABINETS

Pare down the contents of cabinets so there's plenty of space for what's in there. You should be able to see and reach exactly what you have with a minimum of effort.

Dishes

- Dishes should be separate from edible supplies, even if they share the same cabinet. On one side, put plates, bowls, etc. (and try not to stack different items on top of each other, if at all possible). Bowls should be in a different pile from salad plates, for example, so that you don't ever have to move one to reach the other.

- Put more frequently used dishes, such as cereal bowls and dinner plates, on the lowest shelf of the upper cabinets. Drinking glasses, cups, and mugs should be all together and preferably close to the sink (or coffee pot). If you rarely use salad plates or side plates, relegate them to an upper shelf. If possible, hang cups or mugs on a row of easy-to-reach hooks or a mug tree, positioned outside the cabinet instead of taking up the interior space.

Food

- Group foods according to type and packaging. Dry goods such as rice and pasta should be separate from spices, which should be separate from canned goods, which should be separate from boxes and bottles, etc.

- Seal open bags and packages with rubber bands, twist ties, or even tape; or put the contents into plastic tubs or glass jars. Leaving an open bag of rice, even if you think you'll remember that it's sitting upright and not sealed, is just asking for trouble. Without question, one day it will spill.

YOU'LL THANK YOURSELF LATER

If you find yourself stacking dishes due to limited space, you may want to buy one of the many types of dish organizers available at house- and kitchenware stores. One of my favorites is a "Z" shaped unit that allows you to create multiple levels for dishes so that you don't have to pile different types of dishes on top of each other. Some also feature hooks for coffee cups.

QUICK n' PAINLESS

Utensils

▤ Ruthlessly sort through your utensil drawers: discard clutter and never-used gadgets such as melon-ballers, butter curlers, far too many spoons or forks, and especially those things that you can't even identify! Gather rarely used items such as cookie cutters together in a bag or box, and store them on a high shelf or at the back of a lower cabinet.

▤ Arrange your main eating utensil drawer so knives, forks, and spoons are at hand in a utensil tray, not overflowing their compartments. If you don't have a separate drawer for cooking utensils, loosely place them in the remaining drawer space in one layer, with everyday items such as vegetable peelers, spatulas, and serving spoons closest to the front.

▤ Large utensils such as rubber scrapers, slotted spoons, spatulas, and ladles can be stored upright in a ceramic utensil pot on top of the counter.

Cleaning Supplies

▤ Group cleaning supplies under the sink or in the pantry. Don't ever mix them with food supplies. It's a good idea to put cleanser, window cleaner, floor cleaner, brushes, sponges, etc. into a plastic basin under the sink. The container keeps them from migrating among your other kitchen supplies, and the basin lets you pull the whole thing out and select the implements you need without rummaging under the counter.

ORGANIZING THE COUNTERTOP AND WORK AREA

Your countertop work space is the most important area of the lazy kitchen. If you have to elbow anything aside to set down a dish of hot pasta, you're doing yourself a disservice. Even the tiniest kitchen should have a few square feet of well-lit, clean countertop space.

Appliances

▓ Make sure that any appliance you use frequently, such as the food processor, has a permanent space on the counter. Lugging it out from under a counter or off a shelf each time you need it is not the lazy way. Many cooks leave heavy items such as standing mixers on their countertops. Even though they are attractive and functional, they are probably not used very often. Put them away; and make sure your food processor, toaster, and coffee maker have unobstructed space around them.

Knives and Cutting Boards

▓ Keep your knives right above your main work space on a magnetic knife rack. Knife blocks are also good, but for optimum convenience and the best possible care of your blades, you can't beat a magnetic strip. Wood-backed strips of magnet that are about 18–24" long can be screwed or nailed into the wall, and they hold chef's knives, paring knives, poultry shears, and any other frequently used metal

A good rule of thumb for countertop appliances: if you don't use it at least twice a week, put it away. Ditto for anything that has a cover, such as a quilted blender cover. If you use it so rarely that it collects dust and needs a cover, put it under the counter or in a nearby closet. It's just taking up space that you (the cook; the important one here) need.

utensils firmly in place, right in front of your work space.

- Below your knife rack, let your all-purpose cutting board stay out, flat and ready for use (not your meat one, which can be stored upright on the counter or beneath it). Get in the habit of wiping and cleaning it as if it were the countertop, and don't put it away or turn it upright (unless you have very little counter space). Not only is it always at hand for cutting bread or peeling a clove of garlic, it can serve as an alternate work space, where you can set down a hot pan if necessary.

Storage Containers

- Although an extended set of dry goods containers (such as graduated tins for coffee and tea) can take up too much space on the counter, a set of flour and sugar containers is very helpful if you have space on the counter. You then can dip in a clean spoon if you need some flour for gravy, or grab a pinch of sugar with your fingers for vinaigrette. Avoid heavy, elaborate containers such as ceramic ones with heavy lids. Try a light metal or thin glass container with an easily removable lid, preferably one with an edge that lets you smooth off the top of a measuring-cup full of flour.

- The fruit bowl is one of the few other items that can stay on the counter all the time. Stack your basic, long-lasting supplies of apples, oranges, lemons, and grapefruit here where they serve the dual purpose of being decorations and snacks. Because it's near the cutting board and knife rack, you'll always be able to quickly trim an apple into sections for kids' (and grownups') healthy snacks.

A Few Other Things to Think About

- Countertops should be well-lit, either with under-counter lights, spotlights on the wall, or a well-placed lamp if you don't have wiring for anything else. I find an incandescent lamp to be a warming, homey feature for the kitchen. Try a tall-ish, slender tabletop lamp without a large base. Get a pale shade and a bright bulb to shed plenty of light.

- If you have space, a wine rack is an attractive feature if you actually keep wine in it. Otherwise, it's just wasted space; if you're nursing an empty wine rack on your countertop, you'd do better to fold it up and put your food processor there instead.

- An under-the-counter garbage can is not the best choice for the speedy kitchen. Although it's tidy and out of the way, it's not easy to reach, either to deposit garbage or to clean. The best choice is a garbage container with a swing lid, sitting near the sink or stove. It's easy to reach and easy to take out the bag when full, and the swinging lid ensures that you don't have an open garbage container in full sight.

IF YOU'RE SO INCLINED

If you tend to keep a reasonable stock of wine around, but find yourself without space for a wine rack, you may want to consider having one built within your cabinets. Nowadays, many kitchens are designed with a wine rack fitted directly the cabinet unit. What could be cooler!

A tiny kitchen in a former apartment of mine had no room for either a hanging rack or a swing-out shelf in the cabinet to hold pots and pans. I hammered strong nails directly into the wall next to and behind the stove, and there I hung my large nonstick skillet, omelet/ sauté pan, small and medium saucepans, and a kitchen towel and pot holder. A hanging pot rack full of copper pans might look more elegant, but it couldn't possibly be more functional. If you're using this method, you may prefer to buy strong decorative hooks and hang your pots on those instead of on bare nail heads.

ORGANIZING THE COOKTOP AND POTS AND PANS

Pots and pans should always be stored around or near your cooktop or stove because that's where you'll be using them. Some stoves have bottom drawers that hold pots, but they usually don't have much space. Try to reserve the lower cabinet next to the stove for pots and pans, so you can reach in and grab the item you need with ease. It's also safer to have heavy pans in a low cabinet, so you never risk pulling one down onto your head.

- Ruthlessly sort through your pots and pans, and move the rarely used ones away from the regular ones. Put roasting racks, cake pans, loaf pans—anything you don't use more than twice a week—out of the way on high or back shelves. When you occasionally bake a cake or a loaf of bread, it is easier to take that loaf pan out from a high shelf for that particular use than it is to move it every day so that you can reach your sauté pan.

- Nearly any home store offers plastic-coated metal racks that swing out of cabinets; these racks are ideal for bottom cabinets that hold pots and pans. Put smaller, lighter saucepans toward the front, and then you can swing out the rack to lift bigger, heavier pots such as Dutch ovens or cast-iron skillets.

- If you have the space for it, a hanging pot rack is the fastest, easiest way to get to your cookware. Not only is this the neatest form of storage, but after washing, you can return the pots to the rack to drip dry.

- Group your frequently used supplies—such as the salt shaker, the pepper mill, and the olive or cooking oil can—on the counter near the cooktop where they're always at hand for seasoning and sautéing. Although you can keep the dinner-table salt shaker here, you can instead fill a small bowl or dish with salt as chefs do, and then grab a small handful to salt a pot of boiling pasta water or a pinch to season a sauce.

- If you have a utensil container to hold your wooden spoons and large utensils, such as a ceramic pot or vase, keep it by the stove. When a pan boils over, you won't have to rummage through your utensil drawer to find a spoon.

- Your cooktop should have easily cleaned surfaces and a backsplash to keep cooking grime from building up. Usually, but not always, sinks and stoves are built or installed with their own backsplashes or a tile section on the wall. If there's nothing but paint behind the wall where you cook, you may want to apply some brightly colored contact paper, which looks surprisingly nice, won't stain, and can be easily wiped clean.

YOU'LL THANK YOURSELF LATER

One way to make cleaning the stovetop easier is to buy yourself a spoon rest. Instead of placing the spoon that is covered in tomato sauce directly on the white cooktop or counter, simply lay it in its spoon rest. Nowadays, you can find them in all shapes, colors, and designs—everything from a sunshine yellow extra large spoon made of pottery to a flat dish painted as a pig.

ORGANIZING THE REFRIGERATOR AND FREEZER

There's not a lot you can do to your refrigerator and freezer in terms of the quantity and quality of storage space, but you can keep firm control of what goes in and out of both.

- Group perishables such as cheese, milk, and leftovers apart from long-term storage items such as mustard and jam. This keeps you from losing a cup of left-over mashed potatoes among jars of chutney, tahini, and ketchup.

- Get used to certain things in certain places—milk out front, eggs in the door or at the back of the fridge (some people think the door isn't cold enough for eggs and store them in the back of the fridge), sodas at the bottom, and so on. This stan-dardization quickly gives you a better idea of what you're out of—and what you have plenty of for dinner—as soon as you open the door.

- Store vegetables only in the crisper drawer. In a per-fect world, they'll all stay fresher and breathe better if they're loose and not sealed up in plastic bags, but I prefer, for ease, to keep most of my vegetables in the bags they came in. That way, not only can you reach in and pull out all the carrots together, but it's also handy if you forget a cucumber for some weeks (my mother doesn't call it the "rotter" drawer for nothing)—it's much easier to lift out the mushy, green stick in its own plastic bag than by hand.

- Store fresh meat on a low shelf, preferably with the package inside a grocery store plastic bag to help ensure it won't leak or drip out onto other food.

- If you don't have an automatic defrost function, defrost the fridge and freezer (as regularly as you can stand to) to keep the refrigerator functioning optimally and stop ice crystals from forming on freezer food.

- Don't treat the freezer as your kitchen black hole. Although there are a lot of foods that are good to have on hand in the freezer, don't freeze leftover bits of food such as casseroles and stews, thinking that you might eat them one day. If it's not enough to make a meal, you don't have a firm idea of when you'll use it, or maybe you don't even know what it was, throw it out.

- Don't keep the fridge or freezer too full, except perhaps at holidays. Half to three-quarters full is optimal for cooling functions and usage. If they're any fuller, you probably have too much and won't get through it all.

Busy cooks don't have time to lift stacks of bowls to get to the dinner plates, to rummage through the drawer looking for the vegetable peeler, and to get on their knees in front of the refrigerator because they're sure there was a jar of mustard in there somewhere. Reorganizing your kitchen for top speed will take you probably less than an hour, and can save you that much time every day when you're preparing meals.

A COMPLETE WASTE OF TIME

The 3 Worst Things to Do with Leftovers:

1. Clutter the fridge or freezer with useless smidgens of leftover food in small cups or tubs, such as half a cup of mashed potatoes or six peas, instead of composting or simply discarding the food.

2. Keep them longer than three days.

3. Reheat and serve them plain, instead of incorporating them into another dish.

Getting Time on Your Side

	The Old Way	The Lazy Way
Clearing the countertop to find a space so you can take out and use the food processor	5 minutes	0 minutes
Taking out dishes and utensils to set the table for dinner	5 minutes	1 minute
Finding the serrated knife to cut bread	3 minutes	3 seconds
Tracking down that last can of tomatoes in the cupboard	3 minutes	30 seconds
Taking out a saucepan	3 minutes	10 seconds
Figuring out if you have any—and locating—cumin	5 minutes	30 seconds

Chapter four

Phenomenally Fast Food! Shortcuts and Tips

Quick cooking can be a little like juggling: Several things go on at once and it all depends on the practitioner keeping the balls in the air and then bringing it home with a bit of style. Make it easy on yourself by thinking through the meal in advance, before you just slap the steaks in the pan. Make sure that the baking potatoes are already in the microwave and the salad dressing is mixed. Carrots can be sliced in the food processor and be simmering in a little water and maple syrup on the back of the stove, while you do everything else.

To make cooking your meals as efficient and quick as possible, follow these tips for swift preparation.

INGREDIENTS

You don't have to have absolutely everything ready before you cook unless you're making Chinese stir fry (in this case, all the work is in the chopping and preparing, and the cooking only takes a couple of minutes). For non-Chinese cooking, I prefer to do only as much in advance as I absolutely have to in order to get started on the cooking. I know that the Parmesan cheese is in the fridge, but I'll take it out when I need it and not before. And if I don't grate it myself, I'll put it on the table with a grater; everyone can grate their own. Sometimes, this lazy technique finds me hurriedly pressing garlic for the salad dressing with one hand while draining pasta with the other, but I don't mind a little rush at the end of cooking if it cuts my time in the kitchen.

Shopping

Let the salad bar at the supermarket be your sous chef on a busy night.

- Although the food processor is the fastest way to chop fresh vegetables, you can swing past the salad bar at the supermarket and buy items such as green peppers, broccoli, cauliflower, tomatoes, and onions already chopped on really busy nights. (Occasionally salad bar vegetables have nitrates on them to keep them looking fresh and colorful, so don't make this a nightly practice.)

- Cooked chicken and ham from the salad bar can be chopped (if it isn't already) and tossed into an omelet, mixed with a little mayonnaise and celery to spread on sandwiches, or put into a quick cream sauce and served over rice.

- For a quick dessert, let chopped fruits and cleaned berries from the salad bar marinate in a little sugar

QUICK n' PAINLESS

Figure out which tasks slow you up and modify them—if peeling potatoes is your dreaded chore, look for thin-skinned potatoes and scrub lightly instead of peeling. Or simply scrub your regular spuds, cut them into small pieces (in your food processor of course), and cook and mash them with the skins on. Add a clove of garlic, minced, directly to the hot potatoes and whip with a little milk. There's no peeling, it's a dish fit for gourmets, and you get extra fiber!

with a dash of liqueur, balsamic vinegar, or orange juice. When you finish dinner, drizzle on a little fresh cream or plain yogurt. In the case of high-priced fruits such as raspberries, buying them fresh from the salad bar may be cheaper than buying them fresh in little pre-packaged plastic tubs.

- If you know you're making stew, chili, or a pot pie, check in the meat department for raw meat cut into cubes (usually marked "stew"), instead of buying whole pieces.

Preparing

It's hard to speed actual cooking times—chicken needs to stay on the grill long enough to be cooked through without a trace of pink, casseroles have to be in the oven long enough to bubble, and cakes have to rise. Instead, the busy cook saves time in the preparation.

- Scissors are often faster and easier to use than a knife and a cutting board. Use strong, clean kitchen scissors instead of a knife whenever possible—snip herbs directly into salads and sauces, and cut luncheon meat, cold chicken breasts, hard-boiled eggs, pizza, fresh mushrooms, and pita bread. (Get a pair that can be cleaned in the dishwasher to keep them sanitary.)

- Use your hands instead of scissors or knives wherever possible—tear up lettuce, crumble firm cheese into a sauce or on top of a casserole, and toss a salad.

A COMPLETE WASTE OF TIME

The 3 Worst Things to Do with Carrots

1. Buy them peeled and presliced so that you have dry, woody carrots.

2. Chop them one by one by hand instead of letting the food processor do the work.

3. Only buy the kind you have to peel and not taking advantage of the slender young carrots (the kind with green tops still attached) that don't require peeling.

QUICK n' PAINLESS

- Chop everything you can in the food processor, from vegetables to bread crumbs to herbs. Use the grating attachment for foods such as carrots and onions for a soup base—this speeds their cooking time as well.

- When using the food processor, make sure you chop fresh vegetables into pieces small enough to cook quickly. Carrots in one-inch chunks can take 30 minutes to soften, but $1/8$-inch thick rounds are ready in 10 minutes.

- When you're having a pasta dish, cook thin pastas such as angel hair—they're ready in three to four minutes.

- Couscous is much faster than rice—if you don't have time to wait for rice to steam, pour boiling water over couscous in a bowl. It sits for a few minutes to absorb the water and it's ready to go.

- If you need to peel soft fruits such as peaches, nectarines, or apples, drop them in boiling water for less than a minute. Lift them out with a slotted spoon and run under cold water. The skins split and lift right off.

- Rinse and spin dry three or four days' worth of various lettuces for salad. Store them in the crisper drawer in a paper towel-lined plastic bag (such as a small shopping bag). They'll stay crisp during the work week, so you can just pull some out for a salad.

- When you make vinaigrette for salad, add the ingredients to a glass jar, cover, and shake hard to make a perfect emulsion.

- If you prefer to make your vinaigrette fresh each night for salad, put the ingredients directly into the bottom of the salad bowl, whip them with a fork, and put the lettuce directly on top of the mixture. Toss well from the bottom.

ON THE DOUBLE

Halve your work by doubling the amount you cook. It will take you a fraction of the time to cook a little extra now than it would take to start from scratch later in the week. Double up quantities on foods that you'll be using again and again.

- If you or anyone in your life takes a packed lunch to school or work, make a couple extra chicken breasts if you're sautéing chicken. In the morning, slice the breasts on the diagonal for super sandwiches.

- When mixing up a vinaigrette, make extra. A double or triple batch means you'll have some on hand for the next night, or some to use as a quick marinade for chicken or beef.

- When you take a chicken out of the freezer to defrost on the counter all day while you're at work, defrost a piece of beef as well. Eat the chicken tonight, and marinate the thawed beef overnight in that extra vinaigrette, to grill or broil tomorrow.

A COMPLETE WASTE OF TIME

The 3 Worst Things to Do While Defrosting Chicken:

1. Let the juices drip onto utensils you're going to use to cook other foods.

2. Defrost on a plate that you later use to serve the cooked chicken (without cleaning it in between).

3. Return it to the freezer after it has already thawed.

After you've decanted your olive oil into an oil container, don't put it away in a cabinet. Keep it on the counter by the stove so it's always at hand. You know what you use regularly—if you're a big hot sauce fan and you find yourself frequently sprinkling it over dishes, leave it out where you can reach it easily. There's no reason to continually open cupboards, either to put away a frequently used ingredient or take it back out.

■ Make double the pasta you need. Toss the extra with a little olive oil to keep it from sticking, and store in a container with a tight fitting lid. The next day, use it for pasta salad (just top with that extra vinaigrette and add some chopped veggies) or heat it in the microwave for a quick supper.

■ Boiled vegetables may not be that exciting if you reheat and serve again later in the week, but grilled veggies, with their smoky taste from the grill, are still delicious. Grill extra, and reheat in the microwave the next day. Stuff them into a pita and drizzle with dressing for a hearty sandwich (add a little melted cheese if you like) or chop and heat in some spicy tomato sauce for a quick pasta topping.

COOKING WITH SPEED

Various tips and techniques will help move you through the kitchen as quickly as possible.

Food that Really Moves

■ Decant olive oil into a stainless steel oil can kept by the stove. Then you don't have to open the cabinet and remove the lid from the olive oil bottle when you just need a couple of teaspoons for the bottom of the sauté pan (also good for adding to salads and dressing).

■ In a pinch, substitute ground ginger for fresh grated ginger. You won't get the same zesty flavor, but you'll still taste a tangy bite from the dried ground version.

- Cutting up fresh chilies slows you down because of the care involved to keep from getting the chili oils on your fingers and utensils. Substitute dried red chili flakes or hot sauce where possible.

- Never waste time peeling garlic. If you don't have a rubber peeler tube, lay the cloves you need on the cutting board and lay the flat of the knife blade over them. Smack the flat of the blade with your fist to crush the cloves. The papery skin lifts right off.

- To quickly mince more than two cloves of peeled garlic, sprinkle some salt over the cloves on the cutting board. Make a few preliminary chops, then drag the flat of the knife blade over the salted cloves. The abrasive action of the salt helps the knife pulverize the garlic and keeps garlic from sticking to the knife. Hold the cutting board over the pan and scrape the crushed, salty garlic directly into the pan with the dull side of the blade.

- Thin cutlets and fillets of meat cook faster and more evenly. Pound thick chicken breasts with your fist for a few seconds to even them out before cooking.

The Heat Is On!

Actual cooking techniques are often less important for speedy cooking than the preparation of the ingredients and the equipment you use are, but there are a few smart things you can do to speed up your application of heat to food.

QUICK 💿 PAINLESS

For mincing only one or two cloves of garlic, always use a garlic press with an attached cleaner instead of a knife and cutting board. Push the cleaner head into the press immediately after you press the garlic. No chopping, no mess!

- Forget your fear of high temperatures. Turn up the heat under meat and poultry cutlets and fillets, and boil water on high! High heat makes quickly seared meat taste better, not by "sealing in the juices," but by "searcaramelizing," bringing out all the natural sugars to the surface where they turn a tasty, crusty brown. (Caution: most nonstick pans cannot be heated when empty—if you sauté meat, be sure to heat the pan with some oil in it.)

- Roast chickens, meat, and vegetables at a high temperature—400 to 425 degrees instead of 350. There may be a little more smoke, but foods cook faster and they taste better with more caramelization.

- If you heat stainless steel skillets and woks over very high heat before adding the cooking oil, they're far less likely to stick.

- Remember to preheat the oven before putting anything in for baking or roasting. The finished food will not only have cooked faster, but will also be much tastier if it doesn't have to heat along with the oven.

Catch the Wave

- Unless you have a microwave that doubles as a convection oven, the only meats to cook in the microwave are bacon and fish. Chicken, beef, pork or any other meat or poultry in the microwave might be edible but sure won't be tasty, because the surfaces won't be browned. Microwaves turn

YOU'LL THANK YOURSELF LATER

Most of us use the stove that fate has dealt us, but if you have the choice, go for gas. A gas stove lets you cook much more quickly and efficiently than an electric one does. With gas, you get instant heat; when you turn it off, the heat beneath the pot goes away immediately. Electric burners gradually heat and gradually cool, and you can't get the instant temperature adjustment that gas offers.

moisture in the food into steam, so they essentially cook from the inside out. Bacon's high fat content means it will crisp up, and fish is good steamed or poached, but other meats will be pallid and tough.

■ Use the microwave to cook fresh vegetables such as baked potatoes, to heat canned vegetables, and to cook frozen ones, preferably in the dish in which you plan to serve them. Corn-on-the-cob can be microwaved in minutes if you leave the husks on. Put fresh vegetables such as broccoli florets and sliced carrots in a little water in a covered microwavable dish, and steam them. Cook frozen vegetables according to package directions, usually in a covered glass dish.

■ Microwaves are great for scrambled eggs, if you're careful not to overcook them. For a fast breakfast with a minimum of washing up, beat 1-2 eggs in a small cup, add salt and pepper and bit of cheese, and microwave for less than a minute, depending on the wattage of your machine. The eggs will puff up into something resembling an omelet. Don't overcook or they'll be dry and tough.

*&%$! I FORGOT TO COOK THE VEGETABLES!

It happens to us all: Everything is ready to go, but you forget to cook the spinach, or rinse the salad leaves, or the kids won't come in and wash their hands. The uptight cook is in despair, but the "Busy Cook" knows

A COMPLETE WASTE OF TIME

The 3 Worst Things to Do with a Microwave:

1. Use it for baked goods (other than the cake and brownie mixes designed for it).

2. Heat breads or muffins longer than 15–30 seconds (after that they get tough and eventually hard as rocks).

3. Put anything metal into it or run it with nothing inside.

If you have the feeling all of your dishes may not be ready at the same time, or perhaps simply for precautionary measures, you can warm the serving plates themselves. Simply place the platter (just make sure it's oven-proof!) in a warm oven for a few minutes before you serve the food. If serving pasta, spoon a bit of the hot pasta cooking water into your serving bowl while the noodles are cooking. When the pasta is drained and ready, dump the water out of the now-warm bowl. A hot dish just waiting to embrace your steaming pasta—it's magic!

how to successfully keep food waiting. In any case, in the lazy kitchen, it's not so vital that the thing that takes longest to cook goes out first if something else can be cooked and can sit without being ruined.

- Turn the oven on to 140 degrees to keep cooked meat warm, in the cooking pan or serving dish, or even on individual plates. It might dry out a bit if you keep it warming longer than 15 to 20 minutes, but slightly dry is better than cold and hard.

- Mashed potatoes stay hot in a covered pan for up to an hour. Mash them swiftly, then pour on a thin layer of milk, and clap a lid on top. Put them at the back of the stove while you finish preparing the rest of the meal. When ready to serve, stir the milk into the spuds.

- Steam rice so that you don't have to pay any attention to it on the stovetop: bring 1 cup of rice, 2 cups of water, and a pinch of salt to a rapid boil in a covered pot; then turn off the heat (or put it on the absolute lowest heat) and leave it on the burner to steam. Don't stir or remove the lid (not even once!). The rice absorbs all the water and is perfectly cooked in 20 to 30 minutes.

- Toss pasta with a few tablespoons of olive oil or noodles with a knob of butter if the food needs to wait. The oil coats the noodles, and keeps them separate—not sticky or gummy.

- Put a lid or some foil on a casserole and leave it in the oven, which you have turned off. The covering keeps the gravy from forming that lacy crust around the edge.

- If cooked vegetables must be kept waiting, remove them from the cooktop and let them get cold. Keeping them warm in the oven or on top of the stove turns even the firmest carrot to mush. Reheat them swiftly in the microwave or, if they're in liquid (peas or corn, for example), quickly reheat them in their saucepan over a hot burner.

CHILL WITH THE GRILL

With the advent of gas grills, outdoor grilling has become less of a summertime treat and more of a tasty, quick way to cook meat on any regular weekday. I'll always take a gas grill over charcoal. Neat, quick, and easy, gas grills encourage you to step outside and grill; charcoal grills make you think, "I'd rather cook it on the burner than clean out that ash and light a fire."

The open flame makes mundane cuts of meat taste like a celebration, and grilling on a gas grill is a remarkably lazy technique—just slap it on and let it sizzle.

- Preheat gas grills for 10 minutes for fast, even cooking. If you remove the grill rack while preheating, foods are less likely to stick.

- Brush the grill rack with oil before laying foods on to prevent sticking and make for easier clean-up later.

- Make hamburgers thin and even for fastest grilling, but it's easier to keep the center of steaks rare and juicy if they're at least ¾-inch thick.

A COMPLETE WASTE OF TIME

The 3 Worst Things to Do with Sprayable Fats:

1. Forget to use them to grease baking sheets, roasting pans, and sauté pans.

2. Spray too thinly so that they're ineffective.

3. Spray without proper ventilation, causing you to inhale the contents.

■ Precook chicken pieces in the microwave before finishing them on the grill. Be sure to separate the thighs and drumsticks.

■ If you are grilling outside, make the whole meal there instead of running back and forth to the kitchen. Corn-on-the-cob grills in its husk; sliced vegetables, including thick rings of potatoes, can be brushed with oil and grilled on the outer edges, away from the main heat. Grill a few rings of pineapple or bananas that are peeled and wrapped in foil with brown sugar and butter to eat with ice cream for dessert.

Don't be afraid to change your style and technique in the kitchen in pursuit of speed. Cut corners in preparation and cooking and see which results please you—and which don't. Don't feel tyrannized by the need to cook. It's your kitchen and you're in charge.

Getting Time on Your Side

	The Old Way	The Lazy Way
Making a fresh vinaigrette and tossing it with a salad	20 minutes	4 minutes
Preparing 3 pounds of potatoes to cook	20 minutes	3 minutes
Peeling, chopping, and cooking carrots	40 minutes	10 minutes
Chopping fresh herbs	4 minutes	1 minute
Adding cheese to a sauce or sprinkling over a casserole	5 minutes (grating)	1 minute (crumbling)
Baking potatoes	1 hour	10 minutes

Drip-Dry: Tips for Quick Cleanup

Many of us could cook five-course meals without blinking if it weren't for all the cleaning up. Throwing together a meal with lots of fresh ingredients and shiny plates is fun. Scraping the remains of that meal into the garbage and washing a mountain of dirty dishes is not. It doesn't have to be an utter misery, though.

Paying a little attention to which—and how many—dishes and pans you're using while you cook can save time later, as can the intelligent use of cleaning supplies and equipment. A logical approach to these tasks, and a few shortcuts here and there, can help make the cleaning go faster than the cooking.

WHILE YOU'RE COOKING

- After you use the food processor to chop fresh vegetables such as onions or cabbage or carrots, give the bowl, lid, and blade a rinse under the hot tap and set it in the drainer. Don't unscrew the blade mechanism if you have

Always use wood or plastic utensils on your nonstick pans and replace the pans if the coating wears off. A scratched nonstick surface is worse than a regular "sticking" surface, and it will slow down your cooking and cleaning time.

one that comes apart. Just lift out the blade and rinse all the pieces.

■ Reuse pots or use them for two purposes wherever possible. Don't ever reuse any pan or dish that had raw meat in it without washing it first, but if you've just sautéed a couple of chicken breasts in your non-stick skillet, set them on the serving plates and quickly wilt fresh spinach leaves in the same pan with a splash of water. Lift egg noodles out of the cooking water with a slotted spoon instead of dumping them in a colander, and use the boiling water to quickly cook broccoli florets or fresh green beans.

■ Cover the bottom of roasting pans with heavy-duty aluminum foil. Use a wide sheet and cover the pan from side to side and over all four corners, tucking the foil tightly under the edges. When you roast meat, poultry, or vegetables, the foil is strong enough that you can still spoon up the juices and baste without it tearing through. When you clean up, lift out the foil, making sure that no juices slip out onto your pan, and discard the foil. You should have a completely clean pan—and if anything does slip through, your roaster will need much less wash-ing than it would without foil.

■ A sheet of thin foil is ideal for laying on baking sheets for pizza or cookies. You can grease or spray the foil as needed to keep foods from sticking. When the empty pan has cooled, crumple the foil and discard it. You'll have an entirely clean baking sheet that's ready to go back in the cabinet without touching water.

- If you must bake cakes, always line the pan with waxed paper. Don't grease and flour the pan and then lay in the waxed paper—lay the paper in and grease (or spray) it instead.

- Always bake muffins in paper baking cups. If you are careful not to spoon any batter onto the pan itself when filling the cups (and don't overfill the cups), you should be able to dump out your finished muffins without having to wash the muffin tin.

- Use spray oils and fats for greasing pans and baking sheets, instead of spreading butter or fat with a bit of waxed paper. An olive oil or vegetable oil spray is perfect for a light coating. You can even fill a clean spray bottle with olive oil or cooking oil. You can also buy a baker's spray that has butter and flour in it, for coating cake pans and cookie sheets.

- Keep your dish drainer cleared so you can give dishes you've just used a quick wash. After I drain pasta in my colander, I put the pasta back in the pot and give the colander a quick rinse in hot water and set it in the drainer. The salad spinner is rinsed and drained pronto, so it takes up space in the drainer and not on the counter. When it's time to do the other dinner dishes, these big items are already dry and ready to put away.

QUICK ⬭ PAINLESS

To cut waxed paper to fit the bottom of a cake pan, tear off a square of paper and fold it in half, fold it in half again, and then fold the opposite corners together to make a trian- gle. Lay the point of this triangle (which is the cen- ter of the sheet of paper) on the center of the upturned bottom of the pan and cut the outer edges off to match. When you unfold it, you have a circle that just fits the pan.

QUICK n' PAINLESS

Make dinner buffet-style. Place all of the pots and pans on hot plates and line up on the counter. Make it truly authentic and pile plates and utensils at one end. You can skip the ice sculpture for now.

When you finish using an ingredient, return it to its storage place right away instead of letting it sit out on the counter. Take one egg from the fridge, not the whole box. Measure out your rice into the pan and put the package back in the cupboard. Putting items away not only speeds clean-up time, but it also keeps the counter clear for you to work. By the time dinner goes on the table, you want nothing on the counter but the dishes that you used (and maybe a few spills).

Don't be shy about using paper towels. They're fast, clean, and good for draining fried foods, such as a chicken breast you've just sautéed; wiping up counters and cooktops and hands; or wiping a greasy patch on the floor in front of the stove. If you're concerned about excessive waste, wet paper towels can be composted.

SERVE IT FORTH

Once it's cooked, you have to get it to the table, and if you're not careful, all the time you saved in the kitchen will be used up as you dish and plate and garnish. Serve as quickly and as easily as possible with these few simple tips.

Do away with serving bowls and platters. Dish up plates directly from the stove. This way, you can present the meal attractively and as it was meant to be. It's surprising how often people will eat just what's put in front of them. (Maybe your fussy 5-year-old will actually eat something besides mashed potatoes.)

- Don't save your big serving platter for Thanksgiving. To save on dishes, you can serve all the hot foods on one platter: sliced London broil in the center, mashed potatoes mounded on one side, drained green beans on the other. (Pass wet foods such as gravy or cauliflower in cheese sauce separately.)

- Layer foods that go together in a big bowl or on a platter for serving. Pile rice in a large bowl and spoon the chicken curry over it. Lay spaghetti on a deep platter and pour the sauce down the middle. Pour egg noodles into a shallow dish and ladle the hot beef stroganoff over them.

- It's certainly not the most elegant way to dine, but on a busy night, if only family or close friends are dining, place hot saucepans on a trivet or pot holder directly on the table and let everyone serve themselves.

DOING THE DISHES

The heart of the matter. And yes, there are still some cooks in the late 20th century who don't have dishwashers. The following tips can help make less of a chore out of the job, no matter how you wash up.

By Hand

- Don't ever dry another dish, unless you need it that very second. That's what dish drainers are for. Let

QUICK ⏺ PAINLESS

To avoid having to fill up the sink with suds and squirt detergent on the sponge every time you clean another dish, get yourself one of those sponges attached to a hollow handle. You fill the handle with detergent, wet the attached sponge, and wipe away! The soap automatically comes through the sponge and onto the dirty dishes. And there's another bonus—no dishpan hands!

If you wash your drinking glasses and other glassware in hot water and rinse them under cold water, you won't get spots on the glasses and will save time trying to rub them out before your guests arrive!

the dishes sit in the drainer until they're dry, even until tomorrow morning.

- Use a plastic basin instead of plugging and filling the sink. If you have a double sink, use one basin for washing and one for rinsing. This saves you from turning the tap on and off to rinse.

- Run sponges and dishcloths swiftly over surfaces while washing; don't linger on them lovingly. If you have to scrub, make short work of it with a no-nonsense plastic or stainless steel scrubber (remember not to use metal on nonstick surfaces).

- Following a simple, logical system of careful drainer stacking will help you have all the dishes, from a dinner for four, done in less than 10 minutes. Fill your basin or sink with hot soapy water. Get your trusty sponge in hand. Wash the glassware and hang it off the sides of the drainer. Wash and stack the following in the drainer, in order and from the back forward: dinner plates, small plates, small bowls, serving bowls, utensils. Then clean pots and pans and any miscellaneous items, and balance them on top of the other dishes. Wipe off the counters and walk away.

- If you run out of space in the dish drainer, don't leave the job until later or start drying dishes. Instead, spread a clean dishtowel on the counter next to the drainer and stack clean, wet dishes on it.

With a Dishwasher

▪ Let the dishwasher do what it was made to do. Far too many people pre-rinse their dishes, wasting energy scrubbing away baked-on cheese and crusts. The dishwasher will clean it if you let it. Most dishwashers have a pot-and-pan scrubber setting, but you probably don't need it unless you have seriously baked-on food.

▪ Stack dishes in the dishwasher as you finish with them. If all the food is cooked but you're just waiting for one thing to finish, dish up the plates (keeping them warm in the oven if necessary), and put the empty cooking pots in the dishwasher. It will only take about 60 seconds—because you're neither rinsing nor scrubbing—and it makes the whole job seem far faster and more manageable after dinner.

▪ Don't put fine china, silver, or crystal in the dishwasher. The same tough cycles that get your regular dishes clean without your help may damage your more delicate dishware, including wearing gold and silver patterns off the china, wearing the silver off plated utensils, and leaving crystal with serious spots. However, some dishwashers have a delicate cycle specifically for these items. If you've used all the stuff in the china cabinet for a family holiday or event, fill the dishwasher with all the other dishes and wash them first. Let the china wait, and then fill a load with only the delicate dishes and run them on the china cycle.

A COMPLETE WASTE OF TIME

The 3 Worst Things to Do When Loading the Dishwasher:

1. Overload it so plates lean against each other and bowls fit inside one another.

2. Obstruct the openings where the water comes out.

3. Load in pots that still have food in them—during the cycle the food will spray around the dishwasher and stick to the glasses on the top rack.

I wear rubber gloves when doing dishes and cleaning the kitchen; not only to protect my lily-white hands, but to help me clean much more quickly. With rubber-gloved hands, I'll willingly plunge my hands into all sorts of muck, scraping food off plates, scrubbing greasy roasting pans, and picking things out of the drain—stuff that slows most of us down by just being a bit gross. When I have rubber gloves on, I just don't care.

CLEANING THE KITCHEN

"Men were born without the counter-wiping gene," proclaimed a friend of mine whose husband was great about doing the dishes but not so great about the rest of the cleaning. Unfortunately, there's more to the job than just getting the dishes off the table and into hot water.

- Everyone has to clean the floor sometime, but you can make it go faster if you use a sponge mop with a wringer device on the handle instead of a string mop. Sponge mops can be taken out in a hurry for wiping up accidental spills, and you don't have to put your hands on the wet strings of a mop to squeeze them out. They dry faster, stay fresh longer, and their sponge heads can be replaced as needed.

- A wet-dry vacuum cleaner can help clean the kitchen floor in a hurry, especially if your 2-year-old just knocked over a carton of orange juice.

- Use baking soda to clean off greasy dirt in a hurry. Instead of scrubbing away with some sort of "super grease-cutting" cleaner, sprinkle on some baking soda and wipe the spill with a damp sponge. It dissolves dirt and grime almost on contact, particularly the baked-on kind (like the greasy dirt on the back of stoves and on top of toaster ovens).

- No time (or inclination) to scrub the sink with cleanser? Dump in some baking soda, give it a quick wipe with a sponge, pour some more down the drain, and add white vinegar. It will fizz wildly (as all you chemistry buffs know). Rinse it down with hot water from the tap. The fizzing soda freshens and deodorizes.

TAKING OUT THE TRASH

A compost pile may not sound like the lazy way, but if you have room for one in your backyard (and, better yet, someone to take the material out there for you), it can cut down significantly on your waste.

- Nearly every town in the country now has a recycling system, and this helps cut down waste for us all. Use containers to separate your recyclables in the kitchen: paper here, cans there, and bottles over there.

- Peel vegetables directly into the garbage bin instead of into the sink, so that you don't have to handle them a second time.

- Some kitchen sinks are equipped with a strainer tub over a drain, which serves as a receptacle for organic waste, draining off any fluids to keep odors down. If you have one of these, peel food directly into it.

- Keep a plastic basin handy to collect each day's worth of biodegradable waste. Put in the coffee grounds, egg shells, and toast scraps in the morning, add potato and carrot peels and onion skins while cooking dinner, and dump in miscellaneous organic rubbish while you swiftly tidy the kitchen. It's surprising how much faster this process is than carrying every strip of carrot peel into the garbage. Then…

QUICK N PAINLESS

If your garbage bin is too low for you to lean over comfortably, and you don't have a strainer in the sink, peel food into a plastic basin, tub, or bucket on the counter. See, cooking doesn't have to be back-breaking work!

- Dump the day's waste into the garbage, or...

- Better yet, do the environmentally sound thing and start a compost heap in your backyard. Separating organic from inorganic waste can reduce your trash by an average of 40 percent. Put the compost heap as close to the kitchen door as possible, preferably in a compost container, so that it isn't a big chore to take the garbage out every evening. Taking out the vegetable peelings and organic waste to the compost pile is an ideal task to assign to a child in your household.

- In certain cities, local regulations prohibit the use of in-sink disposals, and in some older houses, your plumbing might not be up to the job. If you can have one, though, an in-sink disposal is the lazy way to get rid of coffee grounds, egg shells, vegetable peelings, and leftover bits of dinner; their adherents couldn't live without them.

CLEANING OUT THE FRIDGE

Better to keep the fridge from getting too full of food in the first place than to have to clean it out, but everyone has to do it occasionally.

- The more jammed the refrigerator is with food, the less efficiently it (and you) will function.

- An open box of baking soda in the fridge is not just a marketing ploy by baking soda companies—it actually helps keep odors down. Rip the top off of a small box and set it in the back, where it will absorb strong food smells.

After three months, discard the soda and put a fresh box in. At this point, your fridge can probably do with a wipe-down. Empty the shelves (throwing away everything you don't recognize any more), and use the old soda and a damp sponge to clean the inside out. Baking soda and water quickly clean dried-on food off the smooth plastic surfaces, and don't leave any scent of disinfectant or cleaner inside your fridge.

Cleaning is definitely the worst part of the job, but approach it with practicality and determination. Make a point of doing the dishes with speed, and try to shave minutes off your time in loading the dishwasher or washing a pile of dishes by hand. And even when you get your cleaning down to a flat 10 minutes, accept help. Even if it takes your spouse 30 minutes to do the same job, that's one night when you'll have your feet up in front of the TV instead of having them planted in front of the sink.

Getting Time on Your Side

	The Old Way	The Lazy Way
Scrubbing a roasting pan after making roast chicken	10 minutes	1 minute
Washing the dinner dishes for a family of four	30 minutes	10 minutes
Drying the dinner dishes for a family of four	20 minutes	0 minutes
Preparing muffin tins for batter	5 minutes	30 seconds
Cleaning vegetable peelings out of the sink	2 minutes	0 minutes
Scraping melted cheese off the baking sheet after reheating pizza	5 minutes	0 minutes

Part 3

Flash in the Pan: Recipes for Simple and Delicious Meals

Are You Too Lazy to Read Flash in the Pan?

1   Examining the contents of your fridge is like a trip down memory lane. "Look, honey, here's some fried rice from your birthday dinner last year!" ☐ yes ☐ no

2   You've tried to convince yourself that you prefer the taste of a pallid, breaded, fast-food chicken morsel made with who-knows-what fillers to that of homemade fried chicken. ☐ yes ☐ no

3   You've considered attaching your car locator beeper to the stove. ☐ yes ☐ no

Breakfast Treats that Last All Week

Very busy people generally eat cereal for breakfast (if they bother to eat at all). But processed cereals are growing increasingly expensive and increasingly unhealthy—they are full of added sugars and fats, and low in fiber and nutrition. And your mother was right when she told you that breakfast was the most important meal of the day. A recent study found that children who ate breakfast before school had higher blood-sugar levels, were more alert, and performed better on standardized tests than children who didn't eat this first meal of the day.

Breakfast can be tastier, cheaper, more satisfying, and far better for you when it doesn't come out of a box, and it can still fit the busy person's lifestyle. A tray of moist, fruity muffins or a flavorful quick bread keeps well and provides breakfasts on the run for days. A microwave lets you make your own breakfast sandwich, in seconds, that beats the fast-food kind hands down.

Irish Wholemeal Breakfast Bread

If you only know Irish soda bread as the sawdust-dry brown stuff that your Aunt Maeve made on St. Patrick's Day, you never had "real" Irish soda bread. In its purer form, this fast-mixing, fast-baking bread is loaded with wheat germ that keeps it moist and flavorful, almost like a tender-crumbed cake. Adding extra germ helps keep it moist all week when well-wrapped, and you can toast slices for the last couple of days, heightening the nutty flavor.

In Ireland, it's the traditional accompaniment to smoked salmon, but if you eat a slice for breakfast spread with butter and a thick jam such as apricot preserves, you'll go out the door whistling "When Irish Eyes are Smiling." You can double this recipe and freeze one loaf, but it's so easy to mix, you may want to simply make a fresh one on Sunday mornings.

Makes 1 loaf

1 large egg
1¼ cups buttermilk

Dry ingredients

1½ cups stone-ground whole-wheat flour
½ cup all-purpose flour
¼ cup wheat germ
1 teaspoon baking soda
½ teaspoon salt

A COMPLETE WASTE OF TIME

The 3 Worst Things to Do with Muffins and Quick Breads:

1. Store them in anything other than an airtight container.

2. Heat them longer than 30 seconds in a microwave.

3. Discard them instead of toasting them or slicing and soaking them in beaten egg and milk for French toast.

1 Preheat the oven to 400°. Grease a baking sheet. Sprinkle a thick coating of flour on a clean surface such as a countertop or cutting board (to knead the bread).

2 In a large bowl, stir together the dry ingredients. In a cup or small bowl, beat the wet ingredients (egg and buttermilk) together.

3 Make a well in the center of the dry ingredients and add the wet ingredients all at once. Stir to combine.

4 Dump the dough out onto a floured surface and knead briefly, shaping into a disk about three inches high. Cut a cross about 1/2-inch deep on the surface.

5 Place on baking sheet and bake for about 40 minutes until it sounds hollow when you thump the base with your thumb and forefinger. Cool on a rack and wrap tightly to store.

6 To slice, break into four quarters along the lines of the cross on the surface. Slice the quarters thickly and serve with butter and jam or marmalade.

YOU'LL THANK YOURSELF LATER

Double the recipe and make two loaves of Irish wholemeal bread. When they're cool, slice one loaf and wrap it tightly in plastic. Put it in the freezer for up to three months. When you're in a hurry for breakfast, just pull out a few slices and toast them straight from the freezer.

For an even faster method, you can mix the ingredients in a food processor, blending the wet ingredients first and pulsing in the dry ingredients until they are just combined.

Most Moist Raisin Muffins

The bran and optional wheat germ, as well as raisins or dates, keep these hearty muffins moist and tender from Monday to Friday. Bake them with paper cupcake holders and keep them in an airtight container.

Makes 10 muffins

2 large eggs

1/2 cup vegetable oil

1/2 cup milk

1/2 cup brown sugar or honey

Dry ingredients

2 cups all-purpose flour

1/2 cup wheat bran

1/4 cup wheat germ (optional)

2 teaspoons baking powder

1/2 teaspoon cinnamon

1/4 teaspoon salt

Sugar for topping (optional)

1 Preheat the oven to 400°. Line 10 muffin cups with paper cupcake holders.

2 In a medium bowl, beat the eggs, oil, milk, and sugar. Add the dry ingredients on top and mix just until combined.

3 Fill the 10 prepared cups to the top. If desired, sprinkle a little sugar on top of each muffin. Bake for 20 minutes, or until they are golden brown.

Carrot Muffins

The grated carrots keep these muffins moist for the work week. And don't worry, I'm not going to tell you to grate the carrots by hand—leave that to your food processor. And while you have the food processor out, mix the muffins in it.

Makes 10 muffins

3 medium carrots

2 large eggs

$^3/_4$ cup milk

$^1/_2$ cup vegetable oil

$^1/_2$ cup brown sugar or honey

Dry ingredients

$2^1/_2$ cups all-purpose flour

2 teaspoons baking powder

$^1/_4$ teaspoon salt

$^1/_2$ cup raisins

Sugar for topping (optional)

1. Preheat the oven to 400°. Line 10 muffin cups with paper cupcake holders. Peel the carrots by hand, grate them in the food processor, and set them aside.

2. Pulse the eggs, milk, oil, and sugar in the food processor. Add the dry ingredients including raisins and grated carrot and pulse very briefly, just until combined. (Take care not to overmix or you'll have flat muffins.)

3. Spoon batter into the 10 prepared cups filling to the top. If desired, sprinkle a little sugar on top of each muffin. Bake for 20 minutes or until they are golden brown.

IF YOU'RE SO
INCLINED

Make these carrot muffins into moist apple muffins. Replace all or half of the carrot with the peeled, cored and grated flesh of 2 Granny Smith apples (or another tart apple).

Muesli with Fruit and Yogurt

Packaged muesli in the U.S. is often a far cry from the whole-some mix of dried fruits, nuts, and grains developed by a Swiss doctor and intended to be eaten with yogurt and fresh fruit. It should not contain added fat, nor should there be a lot of processed flakes and puffs, or any artificial or added sweeteners.

You can make your own muesli from all-natural ingredients that are best bought in bulk from a health food store. The basic proportions follow, but if you particularly like banana chips or dried apricots, add extra ones to your muesli. Stored in a large airtight container, you'll always have a hearty, healthy breakfast on hand. You can halve this quantity.

Makes 20 cups

10 cups rolled oats

2 cups barley or bran flakes

1 cup wheat bran

1 cup wheat germ

2 cups dried fruits such as apricots, dates, figs, apples

2 cups raisins (or 1 cup raisins and 1 cup banana chips)

1 1/2 cups chopped nuts (unsalted), such as almonds, hazelnuts, Brazils, walnuts

1/2 cup sunflower seeds

1 Mix all ingredients and store in a cool place in an airtight container.

2 Serve with milk and/or yogurt and fresh fruit if desired.

QUICK n' PAINLESS

For an even quicker version, you can start with store-bought muesli and bulk it up to your taste with dried fruits, nuts, rolled oats, and wheat bran.

Milk and Maple Oatmeal

You know you ought to eat more oatmeal because it's good for your cholesterol levels and an excellent source of fiber. But the instant kind is low in fiber, high in sugar, and doesn't taste very good. If you try to cook rolled oats the night before, they're unappetizing and gelatinous in the morning.

The answer is steel-cut oats or pinhead oatmeal. Although it usually takes up to an hour of attended cooking time, the following technique of soaking them overnight reduces your time at the stove to minutes and results in a tender, nutty-flavored oatmeal.

Makes 2 to 3 servings

1 cup steel-cut or pinhead oatmeal

3 cups water

1/2 teaspoon salt

Real maple syrup

Milk

1 **Right before you go to bed,** mix the oatmeal, water, and salt in a small saucepan.

2 Bring to a boil, stir, then immediately turn off the heat and cover. Leave overnight.

3 **In the morning,** turn on the heat under the saucepan, stir the oatmeal, and bring it to a quick boil while you pour your coffee. Let simmer 2 to 3 minutes.

4 Put it in a bowl, and top it with maple syrup and milk to taste.

Better Banana-Cranberry Bread

Banana bread is usually so heavy and dense that it's often difficult to bake all the way through. This is a much lighter version that bakes up cake-like. And the bananas help the bread stay deliciously moist and fresh throughout the work week. It doesn't even need butter or cream cheese.

The refreshingly tart bite of fresh cranberries lightens the flavor, but the recipe is just as good without them.

Makes 1 loaf

1 stick (1/2 cup) butter or margarine
1/2 cup sugar
2 large eggs
4 to 5 very ripe bananas

Dry ingredients

1 1/2 cups all-purpose flour
2 teaspoons baking powder
1/4 teaspoon salt
1/4 teaspoon nutmeg
1/2 cup cranberries, fresh or frozen

1 Preheat oven to 375°. Grease a 9 × 4" loaf pan.

2 Using beaters or a mixer, cream the butter, sugar, and eggs until they are light in color and very fluffy (3 to 4 minutes).

3 Peel the bananas and add them whole to the creamed mixture. Blend with the beaters, leaving the mixture slightly chunky.

A COMPLETE WASTE OF TIME

The 3 Worst Things to Do While Creaming:

1. **Rush the job of creaming the butter, sugar, and egg, which won't incorporate enough air to make them light and fluffy and will thus make the finished product flatter.**

2. **Cream in a food processor, which won't whip in enough air.**

3. **Start with cold, hard butter instead of softened, room-temperature butter.**

4 Measure the dry ingredients on top of the creamed mixture. Coarsely chop the cranberries and dump them on top of the dry ingredients. (The light coating of flour keeps them from sinking into the batter.) Mix very briefly, just to combine.

5 Place in the prepared loaf pan and bake for 25 to 30 minutes, until browned on top and a toothpick or knife blade inserted in center comes out clean.

YOU'LL THANK YOURSELF LATER

Double the recipe and use the other portion of batter to make mini-loaves. Fill 4 to 6 mini-loaf pans with batter and bake for 20 to 25 minutes. After they're cool, wrap well in aluminum foil, toss them all into a zipperlock bag, and place in the freezer. Next time you need a quick holiday gift, present for a dinner party host (breakfast is always a great idea, since they're too tired to cook the next day), or a sweet treat for your family, pull one out of the freezer. Wrap it in cellophane or waxed paper tied with a bow for a gift, or pop in the oven for your own treat.

To make a quick blender breakfast even faster, set up your breakfast drink the night before. In a clean blender container, add milk first, yogurt next, and fresh fruit (such as strawberries) on top. (If you're using frozen fruit, measure out 1 cupful and leave it sitting in the freezer.) Don't blend yet. Put the covered blender container in the fridge, and in the morning, just slap it onto the motor (add frozen fruit if necessary and the ice cubes) and whizz until smooth.

Fresh and Fruity Breakfast Drink

"Instant breakfast" drinks take the same amount of time in the blender as drinks with fresh ingredients do (which taste much better). The ice cubes will be pulverized into tiny crystals (let the blender run until they do) and give the whole thing the texture of a creamy milkshake.

Makes 2 shakes

1 cup milk

1 cup yogurt (plain or fruit flavored)

1 cup berries (fresh or frozen) OR 2 ripe bananas

3 to 4 ice cubes

1 tablespoon sugar (optional)

1 Place milk, yogurt, berries, and ice cubes in a blender.

2 Whiz until smooth, taste, and add sugar if desired.

Microwave Breakfast Sandwich

Who needs the high-fat breakfast sandwiches from fast-food restaurants? If you have a microwave, you can make a much tastier version at home. Top it with cheese (or bacon, see sidebar), or eat it plain or with a dollop of salsa. If you don't have English muffins, use toast or—even faster—buttered brown bread.

Makes 1 breakfast sandwich

1 English muffin

1 egg

Butter

Salt and pepper

1 thin slice American or Cheddar cheese

1 Split the English muffin and toast.

2 While the muffin is toasting, break the egg onto a saucer and beat it lightly with a fork. You can beat the egg in a small bowl if you find this step messy, but you're going to cook it in the saucer so it will be flat and round. (Beating it in the saucer saves you a dish to clean.)

3 Microwave the egg, on the saucer, on high for 30 to 60 seconds, until it is just set and a bit puffy.

4 Butter the toasted muffin and lay the cooked egg on the bottom half. Lightly salt and pepper the egg, and then lay the cheese slice on top. Top with the other muffin half and eat immediately.

IF YOU'RE SO INCLINED

For a truly authentic breakfast sandwich, flash-cook bacon in the microwave.

1. Place 1 to 2 slices of bacon on a folded paper towel in the microwave.

2. Nuke the bacon on high for 2 to 3 minutes, until crisp and sizzling.

3. Put the bacon on the sandwich and wipe any dripped grease in the microwave with the paper towel.

(For more than two slices, lay the paper towel on a plate and increase cooking time as needed.)

Buttermilk and Honey Blender Pancakes

Mixing in the blender or food processor makes these tender pancakes quick; the buttermilk makes them rise up light and fluffy. If you don't have buttermilk on hand, substitute plain yogurt and a little milk. If you're using butter, melt it in a small cup in the microwave. Butter will give the pancakes a richer flavor, but the same quantity of vegetable oil is faster.

Makes 10 to 12 pancakes

2 cups buttermilk (or $1/2$ cup plain yogurt plus $1/2$ cup milk)

2 large eggs

4 tablespoons ($1/2$ stick) butter, melted (or $1/4$ cup vegetable oil)

2 cups all-purpose flour

2 tablespoons honey (or brown sugar)

$1 1/2$ teaspoons baking powder

$1/2$ teaspoon baking soda

$1/4$ teaspoon salt

1 Place the buttermilk (or yogurt and milk) in the blender or food processor first, and add the remaining ingredients in the order listed.

2 Blend or pulse for 1 minute or less, just until smooth.

YOU'LL THANK YOURSELF LATER

If you're making pancakes for a leisurely weekend breakfast, store any extras in the freezer in a sealed plastic bag. (Put a sheet of waxed paper between each pancake so they'll separate easily.) On a busy morning, toss a pancake in the microwave, top with butter and syrup, jam, or fresh fruit, and you have a hot, homemade breakfast in seconds.

3 Heat a griddle or nonstick skillet over medium heat and pour a little cooking oil on to grease it. Smooth the cooking oil over the surface with a spatula. Test to see if the oiled griddle is hot enough by sprinkling a few drops of water over the surface. If they bounce, it's ready. If they lie on the surface and sizzle, heat for a few more minutes, then sprinkle some more water on and check for bouncing.

4 Using a 1/4-cup measure, scoop batter and pour a few pancakes on the surface, making sure to leave space in between each.

5 Flip when the pancakes look dry around the edges and a few bubbles rise to the surface of the pancake (2 to 3 minutes). Cook for about 1 minute on the other side, until browned. Repeat with remaining batter and eat hot with butter and maple syrup.

QUICK ☞ PAINLESS

For a quick, handheld breakfast, slather a tablespoon of jam onto one or two pancakes and roll them up. Easy enough to eat on the run!

Getting Time on Your Side

	The Old Way	The Lazy Way
Eating breakfast	0 minutes	7 minutes
Sitting through your first meeting of the morning	Like, 2 YEARS	25 minutes
Length of time from arrival at work to lunch	15 hours or something	3 to 4 hours
Cooking healthy, full-of-fiber steelcut oatmeal	1 hour	3 minutes
Having a hot pancake breakfast on a cold morning	25 minutes	3 minutes
Having a breakfast sandwich on an English muffin	25 minutes (to wait at the drive-thru)	4 minutes (make at home)

seven

Quick-to-Make Quick Bites: Appetizers and Snacks

You spend two hours making a tray of elaborate hors d'oeuvres that are eaten within 10 minutes. Life's too short. Very tasty snacks can be made as quickly as they'll get eaten, either allowing the host to join the party or letting the lone snacker get back to the chair in front of the TV as soon as possible.

The best lazy appetizers and snacks are bowls of something that you can dip something else into. If you have a food processor or blender (if you're a busy cook, you do), you can make a wealth of delicious dips by merely opening a few cans and adding a few spices. Add the extra step of actually cooking something first (such as a quickly microwaved eggplant), and you'll have some very elegant dishes indeed.

If you're serving several different appetizers to a lot of people, don't be shy about purchasing ready-made nibblies. A commercially made hummus or bean dip can look like you made it yourself, if you're the one who dumped it into a bowl and sprinkled it with paprika or cayenne.

A nice bowl of olives with a little dish for pits on the side is almost always emptied. And you can always serve potato chips and dip, tortilla chips and salsa, or ready-made crunchy mixes that have names such as Bombay mix or Cajun Spice mix.

Cheese and crackers, which are not necessarily exciting, always get eaten. Make the extra effort to find something other than the usual slab of Cheddar: a piece of Stilton, a perfectly ripe wheel of Camembert, a well aged chunk of Dutch gouda. Lay some glistening purple grapes on the side and you have a cheese plate fit for a still life.

Many appetizers and snack foods tend to be quite rich, so it's good to offer a plate of cut-up vegetables as well. Instead of spending hours trimming broccoli and cauliflower into perfect florets, buy them ready-cut at the salad bar. Check first to make sure they look fresh and crisp. If you have to cut up vegetables yourself, go for the easy vegetables: cut unpeeled cucumbers into long sticks, slice green and red peppers into fat wedges, and blanch fresh green beans and snow peas, which don't need cutting at all. Buy a good ready-made dip from the refrigerator section at the grocery store. (I try to stay away from the preservative-laden dips in cans that are usually arranged in front of the potato chips.)

When it comes to entertaining, the most important thing the busy cook can do is *not* wear him- or herself out. Save your energy for the one nice dish or dessert, and either make the rest very simple, or buy it. A college professor I knew used to preface her very elaborate meals with a big wooden bowl of potato chips to accompany some predinner drinks. I found her attitude very liberating. She was in the kitchen cooking a very lovely meal, so why waste more of her energy piping taramasalata rosettes onto homemade toasts? That's a lesson that all busy cooks should learn by heart.

The 3 Worst Things to Do
with Bruschetta:

1. Make it out of overly
   soft white or brown
   bread, especially
   breads with sugar
   added. You want
   crusty bakery breads
   or a sliced baguette
   for this.

2. Toast the bread until
   it's too hard, crunchy,
   and breakable—you
   want it just slightly
   chewy.

3. Be too sparse with the
   olive oil and garlic—
   give it a good brush of
   oil and a firm rub with
   the garlic for best
   flavor.

Bruschetta

*If you don't have bruschetta (broo-SKAY-tah) in your life, read
this before you ever make another snack or appetizer. This
Italian toast is the workhorse of my kitchen, and the only
recipe in this chapter where you have to handle each piece,
but it's very fast and worth the effort. Bruschetta is toasted
bread brushed with olive oil and then rubbed with garlic, perfect as a snack or to accompany soups or salads for a light
supper. You can also serve it with any of the dips that follow.*

*It's the ideal way to use up stale bread, from sourdough to
rye to French baguettes (if they're not too hard). Though note
that it doesn't work with sliced white loaves out of a plastic
bag or any bread with added sugar.*

Leftover bread, preferably chewy white or sourdough
  bread from a bakery

Extra-virgin olive oil

Garlic cloves

1   If the bread is not sliced, cut into 1/2-inch thick slices and
    toast in the toaster oven or, if you're making a lot, toast on
    a baking sheet in a preheated 350° oven, turning once (it
    will take 6 to 7 minutes all together).

2   When the bread is toasted, remove from the oven and
    drizzle or brush olive oil onto both sides of the toasted
    bread.

3   Rub surface lightly with a clove of garlic. Cut each slice
    into halves (or quarters, if you have big slices from a large
    round loaf) and serve plain or with dips as a snack, or to
    accompany soups and salads. Extras can be cubed for
    croutons.

Cream Cheese with Pepper Jelly

Guests exclaim how strange this appetizer is, and then everyone gradually tucks in and eats the lot. There's an unusual tradition in middle America of appetizers made from a block of cream cheese, covered with sauce, and served with crackers.

The following pepper jelly version was my first encounter with this high-fat little snack, but I've since seen blocks of cream cheese covered with Pickapeppa sauce, with a sundried tomato spread from a jar, and (especially memorable) with a commercially prepared tapenade, the black olive spread from France. Jalapeño jelly comes in red and green versions, and can be found in most supermarkets.

Makes about 1 cup

One 8-ounce package cream cheese
$1/2$ cup red or green jalapeño jelly

1 Unwrap the cream cheese and lay it on a plate.

2 Pour the jalapeño jelly over the top.

3 Serve with crackers, preferably a very crispy type such as Triscuits.

QUICK n' PAINLESS

I have to thank Tricia Medved for introducing me to yet another version of this cream cheese-based appetizer—this one is served hot.

1. Place an unwrapped 8-ounce package of cream cheese in the bottom of a microwavable glass dish.

2. Cover it with 1 can of chili without beans.

3. Microwave it on high for 3 to 5 minutes until the chili is heated through and bubbling, and the cream cheese is melting.

4. Eat with tortilla chips.

Goat Cheese with Pesto

A slightly more upmarket version of the previous cream cheese covered-with-something recipe, this one starts with a log of goat cheese. You can simply cover it with a commercially prepared pesto and stop there. But much better, and far more unusual and tasty, is a quick lemon-parsley pesto made in the food processor or blender.

I prefer to peal off a few strips of lemon zest with a vegetable peeler and let the food processor do the hard work, rather than scraping the lemon—and my knuckles—against the small holes of a grater.

You can serve this with crackers, but it's best with little round slices of a fresh baguette so you can sop up the pesto and olive oil around the plate. (Yes, you have to slice the French bread, but at least you didn't have to bake it!)

Makes about 1½ cups

1 large bunch flat-leaf parsley

1 lemon

1 clove garlic

¼ to ½ cup olive oil

One 5- to 7-ounce log of goat cheese

1   Rinse the parsley, shake off the water, and put about 2 cups of leaves in a food processor or blender. (You don't have to strip the leaves completely off the stems, but cut off the thicker stems toward the roots. The tender ones up top, where the leaves are attached, can go into the food processor.)

2 Using a vegetable peeler, peel 2 to 3 strips of lemon zest longways off the side of a lemon, and add these long strips to the parsley.

3 Squeeze the juice, through a strainer or your hand to catch the seeds, from half the lemon into the parsley mixture.

4 Peel the garlic and place it, with 1/4 cup of the olive oil, in the food processor or blender.

5 Pulse until finely chopped. Add a little more olive oil if necessary to make the machine run.

6 Place the goat cheese log on a serving plate and cover it with the parsley pesto. Pour the remaining olive oil around the plate.

YOU'LL THANK YOURSELF LATER

Buy the best-quality foods you can afford. Not only do better quality ingredients make better tasting food, but if your supplies look good when you open the cupboards or refrigerator, you'll be more inclined to use them and cook. You owe it to yourself to pick the freshest vegetables, the best-looking meats, the plumpest, ripest fruit in season. If you buy hard, pink tomatoes, you may as well not waste your time making a salad from them.

With so few ingredients, there's not a lot of room for variation when making hummus. Garbanzo beans (chickpeas) are the traditional base, but you can also make versions of it with any white bean such as cannellini or navy beans. The result will have a different flavor and creamier texture but it's also delicious.

Hummus

Although hummus has Middle Eastern origins, it has been absorbed into our culture in the same way as pizza and bagels, and it turns up at lunch counters, at parties, in delis, even at church suppers. It can be a dip or a sandwich spread, it's great with vegetables, and it's delicious on crackers or triangles of pita.

Makes about 2 cups

One 16-ounce can chickpeas

2 lemons

A small handful of fresh flat-leaf parsley

1/2 cup tahini (sesame seed paste)

1 clove garlic

Salt and pepper

Dash of cayenne pepper

1   Dump the chickpeas into a strainer, rinse, and drain. Put the beans into the food processor. Squeeze the juice of both lemons directly into the food processor, through the strainer to catch the seeds, and discard the flesh and seeds.

2   Rinse the parsley and shake off the water. Snip off about 1/2 cup of leaves, including the tender stems at the top, directly into the food processor.

3   Add the tahini and garlic. Puree until smooth.

4   Taste and add salt, pepper, and cayenne as desired.

Chili Bean Dip

An old Southwestern standby, this is a hearty and satisfying dip that never gets tired. You can use practically any kind of canned beans, but rinse them first. White kidney beans, also called cannellini, make a pale, milder-flavored dip; black beans, spiked with a little extra cayenne, make zestier fare. Serve with tortilla chips.

Serves 4 to 6

One 16-ounce can beans (try red or white kidneys, black, or pintos)

1 lemon

Cilantro leaves (optional)

$^1/_2$ cup commercially prepared salsa

1 teaspoon cumin

1 pickled jalapeño (optional)

1 Dump the beans into a strainer or colander and rinse and drain. Place drained beans in a food processor or blender.

2 Place the strainer over the food processor bowl (so you don't get lemon seeds in your dip) and squeeze the juice of the lemon into the beans, discarding the rest of the lemon.

3 If using cilantro, rinse it and pick a handful of leaves off the stems.

4 Remove the strainer and add the remaining ingredients to the food processor. Pulse until smooth.

YOU'LL THANK YOURSELF LATER

If you make extra bean dip, or find that you have a lot left over, store tightly covered in the refrigerator overnight. Smooth a thick layer over a corn tortilla and heat in the microwave. Top with grated Cheddar cheese and a spoonful of salsa and roll for a deliciously beany "wrap" sandwich.

Fake Fondue

With the aid of the microwave, Fake Fondue can be hastily whipped up for a snack, a party, or even a casual dinner. You can serve it in a chafing dish or fondue pot, or set it out in a bowl and simply pop it back in the microwave for a few moments if it starts to firm up.

This beer-based fondue has an earthier, more casual flavor than the classic Swiss fondue, and in some ways is more akin to the beery cheese sauce of Welsh Rarebit. If you like, however, you can substitute white wine and Swiss cheese for a more sophisticated taste.

Make sure that you use a flavorful bottled beer, preferably microbrewed, instead of beer out of a can. The recipe is formulated for the microwave, but you can also make it on top of the stove.

Makes 4 cups

1 clove garlic
2 tablespoons butter
1 pound sharp Cheddar cheese
1 tablespoon cornstarch
1 cup flavorful bottled beer, such as a red ale
Dash of Tabasco
1 tablespoon English or dry mustard (optional)
1 round sourdough loaf or boule

1 Cut the clove of garlic in half and rub the cut side all over the inside of a microwavable glass bowl suitable for serving. Discard the halves.

2 Place the butter in the bowl and microwave on high for less than 1 minute, just until melted.

3 Meanwhile, grate the cheese (use the grating blade of the food processor if desired) and set aside.

4 Stir the cornstarch into the butter until smooth. Add the beer, grated cheese, dash of Tabasco, and the mustard if desired.

5 Microwave on high for 3 to 4 minutes, until the cheese starts to melt. Stir and continue to nuke until the cheese is fully melted.

6 While the fondue is melting, cut the sourdough loaf into bite-size cubes. Serve the hot fondue with a basket of the bread cubes for dipping.

QUICK 🔳 PAINLESS

If you buy pregrated cheese, you can make Fake Fondue that much faster. Most stores sell packs of already grated Cheddar and mozzarella, but if you can't find pre-grated cheese, ask at the cheese counter of your supermarket deli. They'll be glad to grate the cheese of choice for you, usually at no extra charge.

The 3 Worst Things to Do with Dips:

1. Serve hearty dips to your guests before serving an elaborate meal that you've prepared.

2. Save the remains that a lot of guests have dipped into all evening, instead of discarding.

3. Serve dips in one large bowl instead of two small ones, which will look fuller and more appetizing over the course of a party.

Super-Quick Shrimp Dip

If you remembered to take the cream cheese out of the refrigerator an hour before mixing this dip, you can skip the microwave step, but we busy people often forget to thaw or soften ingredients. No problem—that's what microwaves are for. This is a mild-flavored dip that you can make zestier with the judicious use of hot sauce. Serve with crackers.

Makes about 1¹/₂ cups

One 8-ounce package cream cheese

2 ribs celery

1 lemon

¹/₄ cup mayonnaise

One 4¹/₂-ounce can tiny shrimps

Dash of hot sauce

1 If not softened, unwrap the cream cheese and place in a medium glass bowl. Microwave on high for 1 to 2 minutes until slightly softened. Do not overheat.

2 Rinse and finely chop the celery. Add to the cream cheese.

3 Place a strainer over the bowl and squeeze juice from the lemon into the cream cheese, discarding the flesh and seeds.

4 Add mayonnaise to the cream cheese mixture and stir until smooth.

5 Drain and rinse the tiny shrimps in the strainer, and stir into the cream cheese mixture just until mixed. Add a few dashes of hot sauce to taste.

Caramelized Onions

It looks like you went to a lot of trouble when you serve a bowl of these richly flavored slow-cooked onions. As many onions as you like are chopped with the slicing blade of the food processor and slowly cooked (or "melted," as the Italians say) in a skillet with some olive oil and balsamic vinegar.

You must stir the onions occasionally to make sure that they don't burn, but they can largely be left alone while you do something else. The result is a tender heap of caramelized onions that can be served on a sliced fresh baguette, on store-bought melba toast, on flavorful crackers, or on bruschetta.

Makes 2 cups

6 large onions

1/4 cup olive oil

2 tablespoons balsamic vinegar

1 Peel the onions and chop with the slicing blade of a food processor. They don't need to be chopped especially finely or uniformly because the slow cooking will tenderize them.

2 In a large skillet, heat the olive oil over medium heat and add the onions. Cook, stirring occasionally, for 10 minutes, until softened.

3 Add the balsamic vinegar, stir, and reduce heat to low.

4 Cook over very low heat for 45 to 50 minutes, until the onions have reduced to a tender brown mass.

YOU'LL THANK YOURSELF LATER

When cooking caramelized onions, make double or triple the amount needed, and store the remainder in an airtight container in the fridge for up to two weeks or in the freezer for up to two months. Add 1/4 cup to soups or sauces to deepen and enrich their flavor. Put them in a skillet over a sautéed chicken breast and add a splash of red wine for an instant sauce. Stir them into the Fake Fondue and spoon over toast for an easy supper.

You can give peanuts or almonds this same treatment, but leave out the rosemary. Both nuts have a sweeter flavor that's better accented by the cayenne and salt alone. Buy unsalted nuts and roast them according to the directions for the walnuts, but using only olive oil, salt, and cayenne.

Rosemary Walnuts

I've seen versions of these at cocktail parties for years, but I never realized how easy they were to make because the rich, complex flavor has such an impact. The recipe below is for 2 cups, but you'll probably want to double it, at least, if you're serving it to guests. The pungent rosemary fragrance and the nip of cayenne make them utterly addictive. If you put a few servings of these nuts around the room, you'll find your guests parking themselves next to these tasty treats.

Makes 2 cups

2 cups whole walnuts (out of their shells, but not chopped)
3 tablespoons olive oil
2 tablespoons dried whole rosemary
1 1/2 teaspoons salt
1 teaspoon cayenne (or more to taste)

1 Preheat the oven to 350°. Place the walnuts on a jelly roll pan (a baking sheet with a rim around all four sides).

2 Drizzle the olive oil over the walnuts, and sprinkle with the rosemary leaves, the salt, and the cayenne. Toss lightly with your hands or a pair of spoons.

3 Bake for 25 to 30 minutes, until the nuts are toasted brown and you can smell the toasted walnut and rosemary. Be careful not to let them burn, or you'll ruin the flavor.

Honey-Mustard Dipping Sauce for Pretzels

Pretzels aren't something that you usually dip, but this zingy and simple mustard sauce is specially designed for them. It makes a nice presentation when served in a small dish alongside a beer mug full of tall pretzel sticks for dipping. Save any extra to spread on chicken sandwiches.

Serves 4 to 6

1/2 cup mayonnaise (lowfat mayo is okay)

1/4 cup sour cream (or plain yogurt)

3 tablespoons Dijon mustard

1 tablespoon honey

1 teaspoon Worcestershire sauce

Dash of hot sauce

1 Combine all ingredients in a small bowl and blend well.

2 Serve with pretzels.

IF YOU'RE SO INCLINED

You can change the character of this sauce by changing the mustard: try a pungent spicy brown mustard or a milder whole grain mustard. Add more or less as your tastes dictate, and increase the honey if you like a sweeter dipping sauce.

Getting Time on Your Side

	The Old Way	The Lazy Way
Making finger foods for a gathering of 15	2 days	1 hour
Preparing an elaborate, creamy shrimp dip	1 hour	8 minutes
Cutting up vegetables for a raw veggie platter	1 hour	5 minutes
Time spent refilling platters of little individual hors d'oeuvres and canapes at your own party	45 minutes	0 minutes
Time spent in the kitchen while everyone else is watching the Super Bowl	30 minutes	5 minutes
Having a panic attack—just before people arrive—that there's not enough food	15 minutes	0 minutes
Time spent fending off compliments about how relaxed you look and how delicious everything is	5 seconds	20 minutes

Stress-Free Soups: From Simple Broths to Hearty Stews

Soup, hearty, filling, and fast, is the best friend of the busy cook, who can (and indeed must) be able to make soup out of practically anything. Serious soup cooks often say that their best results were matters of sheer serendipity—you just have to look at the ingredients in your fridge in a new light.

One of the best soups I ever had was made from pot roast, green beans, and mashed potatoes from the night before. The meat was cubed and, with the judicious use of a beef stock cube and some black pepper, it became a flavorful, hearty, stew-like meal. The potatoes thickened the stock into a cream, and the green beans added color and texture.

Sometimes, however, the only raw ingredients you find in the fridge are a few wilted stalks of celery and the end of a piece of cheddar cheese. But because you also have onions, cooking oil, flour, and stock cubes, you can whip up a simple and delicious cheese soup. It can be a noncombative recipient of anything else floating around, such as a left-over half-cup of cooked rice or a few croutons that you make in the toaster oven as for bruschetta (see page 92).

Be sure to mine the soup knowledge of other cultures. If you have actual chicken stock instead of stock cubes, a little cornstarch and an egg will turn it into excellent Chinese egg drop soup. One of my best discoveries ever was the frugal Italian habit of adding stale bread to soup. Suddenly a rather thin tomato soup becomes a thick, wholesome potage. Go a step farther and stew the heel of a piece of Parmesan cheese into the soup, and you have peasant food fit for a king.

Cold soups are a lifesaver for the time-pressed cook during the warmer months, especially when served with a plateful of crispy, garlicky bruschetta. You don't even have to take the time to chill the soup in the refrigerator. With a food processor or blender, some fresh ingredients, and the help of a few ice cubes, you can have a light, refreshing soup chilled and ready to eat in minutes. If your ingredients are already cool, you don't even need to bother adding the ice cubes. Eat the soup at room temperature and just think of it as a sort of spoonable salad.

If you want hot soup, you could heat up a can of something, but processed soups can be so heavily thickened with starches that the consistency is almost gummy. For the sake of a few extra minutes, you can make yourself a delicious homemade soup with a fraction of the sodium and fat, and none of the chemicals and preservatives. Hot soups can take a little longer to make, but there are some that can be ready to eat in as little as fif-teen minutes—the quick Cream of Tomato in this chapter will be ready in less than half that time. Add a salad and bread and you have a whole meal in minutes.

Most of the following recipes make five to six cups of soup, which is enough for two people to eat as a main dish or for four to six people to eat as a delicate first course.

COLD SOUPS

Honeydew Soup with Basil and Honey

This light and tangy fruit soup is amazingly simple and makes a refreshing first course for a summer dinner, although it's not a meal in itself. The hint of fresh basil adds complexity and depth to the simple melon flavor; but if basil seems too unusual to your palate, substitute fresh mint. Make sure your melon is perfectly ripe, tending toward over- rather than underripe. Garnish with a dollop of plain yogurt if desired.

Makes 2 cups, to serve 2 to 4 as a starter

1 ripe honeydew melon

1 lemon

1 tablespoon honey

Fresh basil leaves (or mint leaves)

1   Cut the melon in half and scoop out the seeds. Cut the halves into slices and cut off the rind with a paring knife, letting the flesh and juices fall directly into the work bowl of the food processor or blender.

2   Squeeze the lemon juice into the melon flesh, catching the seeds with either a strainer or your hands. Add the honey. Rinse 2 to 3 basil leaves and add them.

3   Pulse the mixture until smooth. Taste and add additional honey if desired.

4   If serving immediately, pour into bowls, adding an ice cube to each bowl if desired, and garnish with additional basil leaves.

Green Herb Soup

The arugula in this fresh-tasting soup adds a nutty, almost spicy flavor that makes it quite hearty. You do need a real chicken stock here, though, so instead of using a stock cube and water, use a good quality canned broth, or better, the resealable containers of broth available in boxes.

Serve it as a light summer supper with bruschetta or a crusty baguette, and a salad of sliced tomatoes and mozzarella drizzled with olive oil. Pour a crisp and fruity white wine and you may feel you've been transported to the Riviera.

Makes 6 cups of soup, to serve 2 to 3 as a main course

6 cups good quality chicken stock/broth

1 cup fresh arugula

1 cup fresh basil leaves

1/2 cup fresh parsley

1/2 cup sour cream

1 small clove garlic (or half of a large one)

Salt and pepper

1 Place the stock in the work bowl of a food processor. Rinse and add the arugula, basil, and parsley, along with the sour cream. (Save a few leaves of the herbs for garnish.)

2 Push the garlic clove through a press into the work bowl (to make sure it gets pureed). Season to taste.

3 Pulse gently until quite smooth but not a uniform green. You want to leave a few recognizable bits of greenery.

4 Serve at once, garnished with a small dollop of sour cream, if desired, and the reserved leaves.

QUICK 🔵 PAINLESS

The distinction between chicken stock and chicken broth is practically nonexistent. Traditionally, stock includes bones and some seasonings, such as celery and parsley, but broth is just the meat and water. That distinction is all but forgotten, so when buying ready-made chicken stock for soups, whether in cans, tubs, or resealable boxes, don't worry about the label. Whether it says broth or stock, soup's on!

Pulse this soup in the morning and leave it chilling, still in the covered container of the food processor or blender, in the refrigerator all day (this is a great soup for the month of August!). When you come home after a long hot day, put the work bowl back on the motor and pulse it for a second to recombine, then serve. Cool, quick, and easy.

Lazy Gazpacho

Gazpacho is the most famous of cold soups, a zesty mix of summer vegetables: ripe fresh tomatoes, garlic, green peppers, cucumbers, and onions. Some people like gazpacho deeply chilled, but I find that the flavors are better discerned if it's made with cold vegetables from the fridge and served right away without further chilling.

"Real" gazpacho is made of carefully diced vegetables which are combined to make a chunky soup with distinctive pieces of vegetable. Made in the food processor, you'll get a slightly less beautiful soup, but to be frank, it tastes the same, and considering that it saves you about an hour of work, it's worth it.

Makes 7 to 8 cups, to serve 4 as a main course

6 medium, ripe tomatoes (don't make this soup if you don't have good summer tomatoes)

1 medium cucumber

1 small yellow onion

1 green pepper

1 fresh jalapeño pepper (optional)

1 clove garlic

1 cup fresh flat-leaf parsley

2 cups tomato juice

1/4 cup red wine vinegar

2 tablespoons olive oil (optional)

1 to 2 teaspoons salt

Freshly ground black pepper

1. Cut the core out of the tomatoes and cut them in half into the food processor, making sure all the juices go in. Peel the cucumber and onion and cut them into big chunks as you add them to the food processor.

2. Core and seed the bell pepper and jalapeño pepper and add the flesh in big chunks to the work bowl. Press the clove of garlic through a press directly into the work bowl (otherwise the coarse pulsing may miss it.) Add all remaining ingredients.

3. Pulse very briefly, checking every few seconds, until the vegetables are finely chopped but not pureed. Taste and add a little more salt and vinegar if needed. Serve immediately.

QUICK n' PAINLESS

For the fastest and easiest way to seed and stem a bell pepper, consider it as a four-sided box. Set the pepper, stem up, on a cutting board, and make one cut straight down, so that the knife blade is just touching the flesh on the inside of the bottom. Turn the pepper and cut three more times, until you have four pieces of pepper flesh cut off. All that should remain is the stem with some flesh around it, the very bottom, and a "cage" of membrane and seeds. Discard all this, and use the four chunks of seedless, membraneless flesh.

HOT SOUPS

Oyster Stew

The utter simplicity of oyster stew, which is actually more of an oyster soup, makes it a friend to the busy cook. Milk and butter are usually on hand in the refrigerator, and the only other thing you need is a can of oysters from the cupboard (which, as we discussed in Chapter 1, you should have stocked full of basic necessities and the occasional odd ingredient such as a can of oysters). For best results, use real butter (don't be tempted to cut the quantity) and whole milk.

Oyster stew is best eaten by itself, accompanied simply by crackers or bread. If you are lucky enough to have access to fresh oysters (though fresh shellfish is a pretty rare commodity for most busy people!) so much the better.

Makes about 5 cups of soup, to serve 2 to 3

4 cups whole milk (or 2 cups milk plus 2 cups light cream)
1/2 stick (4 tablespoons) butter
One 7-ounce can oysters in their liquid
Salt and pepper
Dash of cayenne pepper

1   In a medium saucepan, heat the milk and butter over medium heat until barely simmering, 7 to 10 minutes. Don't let it boil.

2   Add the oysters and all the juice from the can. Heat through, 2 to 3 minutes, over medium heat.

3   Season with salt, pepper, and a hint of cayenne. Pour into two bowls and serve immediately.

IF YOU'RE SO INCLINED

Oyster stew is plenty delicious on its own, but to gild the lily, add a spoonful of dry sherry to the soup just before eating.

Lazy Chili

Huge pots of chili simmer all day at chili cook-offs, but if it's not a contest, why stand in front of the stove for hours? Crushed tomatoes and canned beans are the key to a speedy homemade chili. If you have frozen hamburger, thaw it quickly in the microwave.

IF YOU'RE SO

INCLINED

Makes about 5 cups of chili, to serve 2 to 3

1 small onion

2 cloves garlic

1 tablespoon vegetable oil

1/2 pound hamburger meat

One 16-ounce can red kidney beans (or try black beans or pintos)

One 15-ounce can crushed tomatoes

2 tablespoons tomato paste

2 teaspoons chili powder (or more to taste)

Salt

1 Coarsely chop the onion. Pass the garlic through a garlic press.

2 Heat the oil in a large saucepan over medium heat and add the onion, garlic, and hamburger. Sauté until the hamburger is cooked and the onion is softened, 4 to 5 minutes.

3 Drain and rinse the beans and add to the pan along with the tomatoes, tomato paste, and chili powder.

4 Bring to a boil, reduce heat, and simmer 10 minutes, until sauce is thickened.

5 Taste and season with salt and more chili powder if desired.

There's room within this basic recipe to improvise a bit. Add a little red wine or a splash of that morning's coffee along with the tomatoes and beans. Or keep the cooking pared down and doll-up the finished product with a dollop of sour cream, some chopped onion, grated cheese, and rings of pickled jalapeño. Have your own chili cook-off at home!

Basic Chowder

Manhattan clam chowder aside, most chowders are thick creamy soups that usually contain bacon, have diced potatoes as a thickener, and highlight a particular ingredient such as corn or clams. But chowder also welcomes lots of guest-star ingredients, especially seafood, so add a drained can of shrimp or salmon at the last minute, or toss some chopped frozen cod into the hot finished soup and cook for 2 to 3 minutes before serving.

This recipe will let you make chowder out of a wide variety of ingredients. Once you've made the thick, creamy soup, it's the work of a minute to add corn or seafood or both. Don't leave out the bacon, which provides the agreeable smoky undertone to the creamy soup. The traditional accompaniment is salted crackers or, better yet, small crispy oyster crackers.

Makes 6 to 7 cups, to serve 2 for supper, 4 as a first course

    6 to 8 strips bacon
    1 large onion
    3 large potatoes
    2 cups chicken stock (or water and a stock cube)
    3 cups milk (or 2 cups milk plus 1 cup light cream)
    Salt and pepper

QUICK n' PAINLESS

If you really want to speed up your chowder, grate the potatoes in the food processor. Your finished dish won't be as aesthetically pleasing, but this step cuts the cooking time considerably, eliminates chopping, and makes a much thicker chowder in a shorter period.

Choose Your "Guest-Star" Ingredient

Select one of these ingredients, or mix and match. You can be flexible. Try ¹/₂ cup of corn and ¹/₂ cup salmon—or add 1 cup corn and the whole amount of white fish for a thicker chowder. (If using canned corn, drain it first.)

1 cup corn (fresh, frozen, or canned)

1 small can of clams, with their liquid

1 cup canned salmon

2 to 3 frozen filets of white fish (try cod or whiting)

1 Chop the bacon and onion, and cut the potato into small cubes.

2 Put the bacon in a saucepan over medium heat and fry until it starts to crisp.

3 Add the onions and potatoes to the bacon and its fat, and lower the heat. Cover and cook 5 to 7 minutes until the vegetables are softened but only very lightly browned.

4 Add the stock and milk, and bring to a boil. Reduce heat and simmer gently until the potatoes are tender, and the soup starts to reduce and thicken, about 15 minutes. Season with salt and pepper.

5 Stir in the corn, clams, or fish, and heat through. Serve piping hot.

IF YOU'RE SO INCLINED

For a real San Franciscan treat, make yourself chowder in a "bread bowl"—a popular dish sold at the Fisherman's Warf seafood stands. Take a small round loaf of crusty bread (sourdough if you're being truly authentic), cut off the top, and scoop out most of the bread, leaving a solid "bowl" so you don't have a mess. As you're eating the chowder, rip off bread from the top of the bowl (like you do with the cone when the ice cream goes below cone level) and dunk into the chowder. Can't you just hear the fog horns?

Cream of Any Vegetable

This is another multipurpose recipe, a template designed to help you make soup out of any fresh vegetable in 20 minutes or less. It works well for hard root vegetables such as potatoes, carrots, parsnips, or turnips; and for green vegetables such as broccoli, spinach, cabbage, chard, or kale.

The recipe also works for celery or celeriac, cauliflower, asparagus, and green beans, but don't use softer vegetables such as green, yellow or red peppers; tomatoes; or legumes such as kidney beans, pintos, and lentils.

Experiment and see what tastes good to you, and in general, don't combine more than two vegetables. Potato works well with nearly anything, as do carrots, but strong-flavored vegetables such as turnips are fussier about being paired.

Makes 6 cups of soup, to serve 3 to 4

2 to 3 cups of your chosen vegetable (see headnote)

3 tablespoons butter

1 medium onion

2 tablespoons all-purpose flour

4 cups chicken stock (or 4 cups water and 2 stock cubes)

1/2 cup milk or cream (optional)

Salt and pepper

1 Clean and prepare your vegetable. Peel and cube potatoes, celeriac, or turnips, peel and chop carrots, separate cauliflower and broccoli into florets, slice cabbage, etc. Use 2 cups of harder vegetables such as potatoes and carrots, and 3 or more cups of softer, leafier vegetables such as spinach and cabbage.

A COMPLETE WASTE OF TIME

The 3 Worst Things to Do with Vegetable Cream Soups:

1. Try to combine too many vegetables so that the flavor gets muddy.

2. Make them too thin so that the soup is watery instead of creamy.

3. Forget an appetizing garnish of a sprinkle of parsley or a few croutons.

2 In a large saucepan, melt the butter over medium heat, and add the onion and vegetable. Stir to combine, cover, and cook the vegetables over low heat for 5 to 10 minutes, until softened but only lightly browned.

3 Stir in the flour and cook 2 to 3 minutes. Blend in the stock, or water and cubes, and bring to a boil. Reduce heat and simmer 5 to 10 minutes, until vegetables are tender.

4 Add milk or cream if desired, and puree the soup in two or three portions in the blender. Be very careful when pureeing hot soup and don't overload the blender (fill it less than half full).

5 Season to taste with salt and pepper. Serve with crackers, toast, or bruschetta (see page 92).

IF YOU'RE SO
INCLINED

This soup is even easier to puree if you use a hand-held blender. Simply immerse the blender in the soup and let it rip! Just be careful not to lift the blender motor above soup level or you'll be covered with Cream of Anything.

If you're serving extra bread and cheese on the side, line a baking sheet with aluminum foil and lay all the bread on it, including those slices you need for the soup. Cover the bread with the cheese slices and put the baking sheet under the broiler for 3 to 4 minutes, until the cheese is melted and bubbly. (If the sheet won't fit, put it in a preheated 350° oven for 10 minutes.) When it's time for cleanup, just throw away the foil and you have a clean baking sheet to put away.

French Onion Soup

This classic soup topped with bread and cheese might seem complicated, but by taking a few shortcuts, you can get a very tasty version on the supper table in half an hour.

Canned beef stock isn't ideal by itself, but enriched with red wine and a hint of thyme, as well as onions, it's very good. It's usually quite salty, so you shouldn't need to add extra salt to the dish. For a warm and cozy supper, serve with a green salad and additional bread and cheese.

Makes 6 to 7 cups of soup, to serve 3 to 4

4 medium onions

3 tablespoons olive oil

1 teaspoon dried thyme (whole, not ground)

Two 16-ounce cans beef stock

1 cup dry red wine

4 thick slices Swiss cheese

4 slices white bread (preferably from a baguette or sour-dough loaf)

1 Peel the onions and slice them thinly (or chop them finely) in the food processor.

2 In a large saucepan, heat the olive oil over medium heat and add all the chopped onions. Cook, stirring occasionally, until the onions are softened and richly browned, about 15 minutes. Lower the heat if necessary so they don't burn.

3 When the onions are a soft, caramelized mass, add the thyme, then stir in the beef stock and wine. Stir well, and leave to simmer for about 5 minutes.

4 Meanwhile, place the cheese slices on the bread and toast in the toaster oven or under the broiler, until cheese is melted.

5 Lay each slice in the bottom of a serving bowl, pushing it down to fit if necessary, and ladle the hot soup over the cheesy bread, making sure to get a portion of onions in each bowl. Serve immediately.

Recreate a night at the local French bistro—light some candles and savor your soup with a lovely French white wine. And don't forget the chocolate mousse for dessert! (Store bought—but of course!)

The Lazy Way

Cheese Soup

Like the soldier in the story who taught the villagers to make soup out of a stone, cheese soup is what the busy cook makes when there seems to be nothing to eat. Warm and comforting, it's delicious with hot buttered toast or crackers—much better for supper than simply cold cheese on bread. I've seen similar versions of cheese soup made with Stilton cheese, in which case I'd leave out the hot sauce and maybe add a finely chopped, peeled apple when cooking the onion.

Makes 5 to 6 cups, to serve 2 as a main course, 4 as a starter

1 onion

1 rib celery

1 clove garlic

2 tablespoons butter or vegetable oil

2 tablespoons all-purpose flour

3 cups chicken stock (or 3 cups water and 2 stock cubes)

2 cups milk

8 ounces Cheddar cheese

1 teaspoon Worcestershire sauce

Hot sauce

Salt and pepper

1 Chop the onion and celery. Pass the garlic through a garlic press.

2 In a large saucepan, heat the butter or oil over medium heat and sauté the onion, celery, and garlic 4 to 6 minutes or until softened.

A COMPLETE WASTE OF TIME

The 3 Worst Things to Do with Cheese:

1. Store it in a wrapping that's not completely airtight.

2. Let it get wet.

3. Add it to sauces or stews without first grating it or chopping it into tiny cubes.

3 Stir in the flour and cook 2 minutes. Stir in the stock and milk and bring to a simmer.

4 Meanwhile, grate the Cheddar cheese in the food processor and add it to the soup while stirring. Stir until the cheese is melted.

5 Lower the heat and simmer gently, without boiling, 4 to 5 minutes, until the soup is thickened.

6 Add Worcestershire sauce and season with hot sauce, salt, and pepper to taste.

QUICK ⬭ PAINLESS

When you're really in a hurry, use pre-grated cheese. Either buy a package in the diary section, or buy a half pound from the deli salad bar.

Summertime Tomato and Bread Soup

Like oyster stew, this is another dish where the result is far more than the sum of its parts. This is Italian home cooking, substantial enough to serve as an entire meal with the addition of the poached egg, but light tasting and fresh. Use good bakery bread such as a crusty sourdough. This soup can only be made in the summer, when the basil is fresh and the tomatoes are flavorful and perfectly ripe. Use canned or packaged chicken broth, not stock cubes, for this soup.

Makes about 5 cups of soup, to serve 2

2 to 3 large, ripe tomatoes

2 cloves garlic (1 to be reserved for rubbing on the bread)

Extra-virgin olive oil

3 cups chicken stock

Salt and pepper

Pinch of red chili flakes

2 slices sourdough bread

2 large eggs

Fresh basil

1 Cut the tomatoes into large chunks. Pass 1 clove of garlic through a garlic press.

2 In a large saucepan, heat 2 tablespoons olive oil over medium heat. Add the tomatoes and minced garlic and cook 3 to 4 minutes, until the tomatoes soften and the garlic smells pungent.

IF YOU'RE SO
INCLINED

If you have an aversion to tomato seeds in your soup, or perhaps choose to make this a more elegant dish, seed the tomatoes before chopping. Simply cut in half and squeeze out the seeds. Then chop the flesh and add to the soup.

3 Add the chicken stock and season with salt and pepper and chili flakes. Bring to a gentle simmer.

4 While the soup is simmering, toast the bread and brush it with olive oil. Rub the remaining clove of garlic over the surface. Lay each slice of bread in the bottom of a serving bowl.

5 Break the two eggs onto the surface of the simmering soup, cover the pot, and leave for 3 to 4 minutes to poach.

6 While the eggs are poaching, rinse a good handful of fresh basil leaves, shake dry, and tear up.

7 Using a slotted spoon, lift each egg out of the soup and place on the bread. Stir the basil into the soup and pour the soup over the bread and eggs. Serve immediately.

QUICK ☞ PAINLESS

Skip the step of brushing the bread with olive oil and rubbing it with garlic. Simply toast thick slices and put them in the bottom of the bowl—you'll be eating in minutes.

White Bean and Spinach Stew

Inspired by hearty Tuscan bean dishes, this fragrant and filling stew provides an entire meal in a bowl. It fills the house with the inviting scents of garlic and sausage, and—Mama mia!— it's ready in about 15 minutes.

The Italian habit of thickening stews with white bread is fast and frugal, but don't put bread in the stew if you only have regular white sandwich bread. You need a good, chewy bakery bread to achieve the proper texture.

Makes 6 to 8 cups of stew, to serve 4 as a main course

2 links sweet Italian sausage

1 onion

2 cloves garlic

1 pound fresh spinach leaves, or one 10-ounce package frozen

1 tablespoon olive oil

4 cups water

2 chicken stock cubes

One 16-ounce can cannellini (white kidney beans) or pintos

1 teaspoon dried sage (optional)

$1/2$ teaspoon red chili flakes

1 teaspoon salt

2 slices stale white bread (preferably sourdough or chunks of a baguette)

Parmesan cheese (optional)

YOU'LL THANK YOURSELF LATER

Slice and store the ends of stale loaves of crusty white bakery breads, such as sourdough boules and French baguettes, in a zipper-lock plastic bag in the freezer. If you need to thicken a soup with crumbled bread, such as in this recipe, or toast bread for soup as in the French Onion Soup (see page 118) or Summertime Tomato and Bread Soup (see page 122), use these frozen slices straight from the freezer.

1. Coarsely chop the Italian sausage and onion into small chunks. Pass the garlic through a garlic press. If you're using fresh spinach, rinse it well to remove any grit, and leave it whole.

2. In a large saucepan, heat the olive oil over medium heat and add the sausage, garlic, and onion. Sauté until sausage is cooked and onion is softened and lightly browned. Pour the water into the pan and add the stock cubes.

3. Drain the can of beans (through a strainer or by holding the lid you just removed over the can opening and pouring into the sink) and add beans to the sausage. Add the fresh or frozen spinach, the sage if using, and the chili flakes and salt.

4. Raise the heat slightly and bring to a simmer. While the pot is heating, crumble the bread into the soup. Stir well. Let the soup simmer for about five minutes. Taste and adjust seasonings. Serve immediately, dusted with Parmesan if desired. (This soup is best eaten fresh and not stored.)

IF YOU'RE SO INCLINED

To dress this dish up a bit, and make the flavor richer and more mellow, replace 1 cup of the water with 1 cup of dry white wine. Make sure to pour a glass to drink with it, as well!

Homemade Cream of Tomato

The fresh taste of this soup, made of canned tomatoes and milk, cannot be equaled by canned cream of tomato, where the flavor is often masked by thickeners and too much salt. It's wonderful for lunch on a cold wintery day.

The bit of baking soda in the soup keeps the acidic tomato from curdling the milk. Be sure you level off the 1/4 teaspoon so you're not adding any more than that, or you'll make the finished soup completely non-acidic (and therefore bland). Serve with crackers and, if you like, a small pat of butter floating on the surface of each bowl.

Makes about 5 cups of soup, to serve 2 to 3

One 16-ounce can whole plum tomatoes
1/4 teaspoon baking soda
2 1/2 to 3 cups milk
Salt and pepper
Dash of cayenne pepper or hot sauce (optional)

1 In a large saucepan, place the tomatoes and their juice over medium heat and break the tomatoes into small bits with a knife and fork or a potato masher.

2 When the tomatoes have come to a boil, reduce the heat and add a pinch of baking soda, no more than 1/4 teaspoon. The tomatoes will foam up. Stir until the foam subsides.

3 Slowly stir in the milk and heat until just simmering. Do not boil the milk. Season with salt and pepper, and a dusting of cayenne or dash of hot sauce, if desired, and serve immediately.

Getting Time on Your Side

	The Old Way	The Lazy Way
Making and chilling a cold soup for a summer supper	8 hours	10 minutes
Cooking onions and making stock to make a rich bowl of French Onion Soup	3 hours	30 minutes
Concocting a spicy pot of homemade chili	1½ hours	15 minutes
Cooking up a cream of tomato soup from scratch	1 hour	10 minutes
Preparing beans for a bean soup or stew	10 hours (soaking and cooking)	1 minute (open a can)
Time spent on a snowy day making a hearty chowder before you can join the kids in the front yard to make a snowman	2 hours	15 minutes

Chapter
nine

Ready-in-Minutes
Red Meat

Thin is in when it comes to meat; and, in some ways, the busy carnivore has an easier time creating dinner: meat, starch, veg, and you're done. For many people, it's not dinner unless there's a central piece of protein on the plate, and it can be a surprisingly quick way to pull together a meal.

Steaks, happily, taste best when they're cooked quickly over a relatively high heat. Thin-cut meats, such as veal medallions or minute steaks, are always a fast choice. Minute steaks are pieces of sirloin or chuck that have been run through a mechanical meat pounder by the butcher. They must be sautéed at top speed and eaten medium-rare, otherwise the meat will turn tough and inedible. Eat them plain or with any of the steak toppings in this chapter. You can buy minute steaks at the supermarket, or you can beat your own if you've got beef in the fridge and have had a bad day at the office. If you've had a really bad day, you can grind your own hamburger, but for regular days, just buy the leanest ground beef you can find.

Pork tenderloin, thin when sliced into medallions, can be swiftly sautéed and covered in a sauce for a slightly fancy meal, while thin pork chops cook through in 6 to 8 minutes for a simple family supper. Both pork and beef are available in meat departments already cut into cubes and usually marked "stew." While beef cut into stew pieces usually needs a little longer cooking time to be tender, pork cubes (which are cheaper, too) can be made into a spicy curry in about 25 minutes, with only about 5 minutes of prep time.

Ham can be a good choice because it is usually sold already cooked, as with canned picnic hams. They may not be gourmet fare, but one will last in the fridge for several meals: sliced with mustard sauce at dinner; packed in brown-bag lunches; diced in omelets or scrambled eggs, salads, casseroles, and pasta dishes. Sausages can also be quick and easy for busy nights. Polish kielbasa is a handy choice because it's already cooked and only needs to be heated through.

Meat of any kind on a dinner plate usually requires a starch, but boiling the potatoes that many of us expect alongside can take too long for the following quick-cooking meats. If you have a microwave, you can have baked potatoes ready for four people in 10 minutes. Just scrub the spuds and be sure to prick them with a fork first, or they could explode in the microwave. Other good starch options are rice, which can mind itself while you finish the rest of dinner, pasta, or noodles. Add a vegetable, and dinner is ready in minutes.

Hamburger Stroganoff

When I was young, my mother fed us hamburger in all manner of disguises, but few were as successful as hamburger prepared according to a streamlined method for Beef Stroganoff. It's tastiest served with egg noodles. Or resort to another of my mother's developments and spoon the stroganoff over toast.

Serves 4

1 pound lean hamburger

1 onion

1 clove garlic

1 tablespoon tomato paste

1 tablespoon all-purpose flour

3/4 cup water

1 beef stock cube

Salt and pepper

1/2 cup sour cream

1   In a large skillet, sauté the hamburger over medium heat. While the hamburger is cooking, slice the onion.

2   Push the garlic through a garlic press directly into the meat. Add the onion. Sauté until the onions have softened and are lightly browned.

3   Blend the tomato paste into the meat and sprinkle the flour over all. Stir to combine, then slowly blend in the water.

4   Add the stock cube and bring the mixture to a boil, breaking up the stock cube, which will melt as the water heats.

5   Cook 3 to 4 minutes, and then taste and season with salt and pepper. Blend in the sour cream and heat through.

Believe it or not, you just made a delicious Russian classic with a $1.19 package of hamburger and some ingenuity. Blow all the money you saved on meat by going out to the video store and renting *Dr. Zhivago*!

The Lazy Way

The steaks will be much more tender and cook more quickly if you take a few moments to beat them with a meat mallet or roll or beat them lightly with rolling pin. Lay a piece of plastic wrap over the steak before hitting it, and you won't have to wash your mallet or rolling pin. It's also a good way to take out some aggression after a hard day at work.

Steaks with Mushroom Sauce

Mercifully, quick-cooking actually suits some tougher cuts of meat such as flank steak or London Broil (which is usually a big piece of sirloin). If you overcook these cuts, you get a tough, flavorless meal, but a quick sauté in a very hot pan leaves them succulent and tender. The mushroom sauce is an easy topping and goes nicely with mashed potatoes, too, but this basic method of steak cooking will serve you well, no matter what the topping.

Serves 2

1 tablespoon cooking oil

2 fillets of beef, no more than 3/4-inch thick (either sirloin or flank steak)

Salt and pepper

8 ounces fresh white mushrooms

1 tablespoon butter

1 clove garlic

1/4 cup white wine

2 tablespoons cream (optional)

1. Heat an empty heavy skillet, preferably cast iron and not a nonstick pan, over high heat for several minutes. Add the cooking oil and lay the steaks in the pan. Salt and pepper them.

2. Cook over high heat for 4 to 5 minutes, then turn and cook another 4 to 5 minutes for a medium steak.

3. While the steak is cooking, slice the mushrooms.

4 Remove the steak from the pan to a plate and allow the meat to rest for a couple of minutes while you make the sauce. (Resting allows the tensed-up, just-cooked meat fibers to relax and taste more tender.)

5 Reduce the heat to medium and add the butter to the pan. Press the garlic clove into the butter and sauté for about 30 seconds.

6 Add the sliced mushrooms and cook for 4 to 5 minutes, stirring occasionally, until all the liquid evaporates.

7 Pour in the white wine, cook for 1 to 2 minutes, and then stir in the cream if using. Season with salt and pepper and pour over the steak. Serve immediately.

Other Toppings for Steak

Herbal butter: Blend a couple of tablespoons of chopped fresh parsley and chives with a couple of tablespoons of softened butter and a teaspoon of lemon juice. Add half a clove of minced garlic, if desired.

Red wine sauce: Add 1/4 cup red wine and 2 tablespoons of butter to the pan juices after removing the steaks. Pour any liquid from the steaks as they rest back into the pan and season strongly with black pepper. Drizzle over the steak just before serving.

Bleu cheese sauce: Blend 2 tablespoons of crumbled bleu cheese with 1/4 cup of sour cream and a tablespoon of lemon juice.

IF YOU'RE SO
INCLINED

Rub thin fillets of beef or pork with garlic salt or Italian herbs before cooking them for an extra burst of flavor.

Stir-Fried Beef with Snow Peas

Flank steak is an underrated cut of beef, perhaps because some cooks treat it like a T-bone, and then it's tough and chewy. It needs to be quickly cooked and served right away to be tender, and a stir-fry is ideal.

This one is particularly fast because you don't have to prep and blanch a vegetable. Snow peas require very little handling and no precooking for a stir-fry, unlike broccoli. If you buy them from a salad bar, they'll already be topped and tailed and washed. This dish cooks very quickly, so make sure you start the rice before you even slice up the meat.

Serves 4

1 pound flank steak

3 tablespoons soy sauce

1 teaspoon cornstarch

2 cloves garlic

3 scallions

2 tablespoons vegetable oil

2 cups snow peas

1/2 cup water

1/2 of a chicken stock cube

1 teaspoon dark sesame oil

1 Slice the flank steak into thin pieces, cutting against the grain of the meat, and combine in a bowl with the soy sauce. Leave to marinate for 10 minutes.

2 Meanwhile, in a small cup, mix the cornstarch with 2 tablespoons of cold water and set aside. Pass the garlic through a garlic press, and chop the green part of the scallions.

Slice the beef the night before you plan to use it, and leave it in the marinade overnight and all day long. It will have picked up a strong soy sauce flavor, so go easy on the soy sauce when you're seasoning the finished dish.

3   Heat the oil in a wok over high heat, until it just starts to smoke (you can also cook this in a nonstick skillet but keep the heat a little lower for the good of the pan). Add the beef (it will have absorbed most of the soy sauce) and garlic and stir-fry until the beef is just starting to brown, about 3 minutes.

4   Add the snow peas and scallions and stir-fry for 1 to 2 minutes. Pour in the water and add the half stock cube and the sesame oil. Bring to a boil and pour in the cornstarch-water mixture. Stir well until the mixture thickens, which will be right away.

5   Serve immediately over white rice, with extra soy sauce on the side if desired.

YOU'LL THANK YOURSELF LATER

To cut your flank steak enviably thin for a stir-fry, start with a frozen piece. Take it out of the freezer in the morning when you plan to use it that night, and leave it in the refrigerator all day to thaw. It should still be slightly frozen and fairly firm when you take it out that evening, which will allow you to cut it very thin with a sharp knife.

Beef Fajitas

Fajitas might sound complicated, but if you've got store-bought tortillas, store-bought salsa, ready-grated cheese, and sour cream, if you like, you can plunk them on the table and let everyone assemble their own. All you need to do is cook the meat (and you can use chicken instead of beef).

Serve a green salad on the side to add a little vegetation to your meal.

Serves 4

1¹/₂ pounds round steak

1 green pepper

1 onion

2 tablespoons vegetable oil

8 tortillas (corn or flour)

1 lime (or lemon)

Toppings

Grated Cheddar cheese

Salsa

Sour cream (optional)

1 Slice the beef, pepper, and onion into thin strips.

2 In a large skillet, heat the oil over medium-high heat. Add meat, pepper, and onion. Sauté 6 to 8 minutes, until the meat is well browned and cooked through and the vegetables start to soften.

QUICK ᴵᴺ PAINLESS

To make things even faster, buy presliced beef specifically for fajitas, which you'll find in the meat section at many supermarkets (sometimes with a lemon or lime in the package—ugh! throw that away). It makes a warm and substantial meal without a lot of effort.

3 While the meat is cooking, heat the tortillas in the microwave, if desired. Wrap the tortillas in a clean kitchen towel or in plastic wrap. Lay the wrapped tortillas on a plate and heat them in the microwave on high for 45 seconds.

4 Place all the toppings on the table.

5 Squeeze the lime (or lemon) juice over the meat mixture. Season with salt and pepper, place in a bowl, and serve immediately.

IF YOU'RE SO
INCLINED

To make tacos, use ground beef instead of steak. While cooking the ground beef, add 1 teaspoon of chili powder to it. Mince the pepper and onion instead of slicing. Use taco shells if you're after something crunchy, or stick with the tortillas for soft tacos.

Veal Piccata

Thin strips of veal cook in record time, and the piccata topping of lemon juice and capers (piccata means "sharp") makes a very elegant dish in 8 or 9 minutes. Have pasta or baked potatoes, and some steamed asparagus or broccoli ready to go before you even start cooking the veal. Veal is usually found in thin scallops, but beat the pieces thin with a mallet if they're thicker than 1/2-inch. This same recipe works well with thin chicken breasts.

Serves 2

2 veal scallops, 6 to 8 ounces each

1/2 cup bread crumbs

Salt and pepper

1 tablespoon butter

2 tablespoons olive oil

1 lemon

2 tablespoons capers

1   Dip the veal scallops in the bread crumbs, pressing so they adhere. Sprinkle with salt and pepper.

2   In a medium nonstick skillet, melt the butter and olive oil together over medium heat.

3   Add the breaded veal scallops to the pan and cook 3 to 4 minutes on each side until they're golden. Watch carefully to make sure that the bread crumbs don't burn.

4   Halve the lemon and squeeze the juice over the veal. Add the capers, heat very briefly, and serve immediately.

A COMPLETE WASTE OF TIME

The 3 Worst Things to Do with Veal:

1. Overcook it so it's tough and tasteless.

2. Smother it in a heavy sauce that drowns its delicate flavor.

3. Serve it at a vegetarian convention.

Pork Medallions in Beer and Mustard

If you can find pork already cut into medallions, buy them, or ask the butcher to slice the pork tenderloin into medallions for you. Use a good, full-bodied beer such as Samuel Adams Boston Ale.

Serves 4

1 1/2 pounds pork tenderloin

Flour for dusting

Salt and pepper

2 to 3 tablespoons olive oil

1 cup full-bodied beer

2 tablespoons Dijon mustard

1/2 teaspoon dried thyme

1/4 to 1/2 cup light cream

1 If your tenderloin is whole, slice it on the diagonal into thin medallions. Dust generously with flour and sprinkle with salt and pepper.

2 In a large nonstick skillet, heat the olive oil over high heat and quickly sauté all the medallions, turning them, for 3 to 4 minutes until they are well browned.

3 Pour in the beer, blend in the mustard, and add the thyme. Reduce the heat and simmer for 8 to 10 minutes.

4 Add the cream and generously season with salt and lots of black pepper. Simmer another 5 minutes and serve.

YOU'LL THANK YOURSELF LATER

The hearty nature of this sauce makes it a good dish for freezing. Make a double batch, and let half of it cool. Freeze the cooled half in a gallon-size zipperlock freezer bag. Later, you can unbag it into a shallow casserole to thaw and reheat in the microwave.

Pork Chops with Apples and White Wine

I was brought up to believe that pork had to be nearly inciner-ated to prevent trichinosis, and I couldn't believe it when I married a man who quickly sizzled pork chops and tossed them on a dinner plate. But it's true—pork chops 1/2 to 3/4-inch thick will cook as quickly as 8 to 12 minutes.

Serves 4

2 apples

4 pork chops, 1/2 to 3/4-inch thick

Salt and pepper

1 tablespoon butter

1/2 cup white wine (or 1/2 cup apple juice plus 1 teaspoon cider vinegar)

1. Core the apples, peel if desired, and cut into thin slices. Season the chops with salt and pepper.

2. In a large skillet, melt the butter over medium-high heat. Add the chops and cook 2 to 3 minutes until they are browned on one side.

3. Turn the chops and add the apples to the pan. Cover. Cook 7 to 8 minutes until the chops are cooked through and the apples soften. Place the chops on a serving platter.

4. Turn the heat to high and pour the wine (or juice and vine-gar) over the apples and deglaze the pan. Bring to a boil over high heat and cook several minutes until the liquid is slightly reduced.

5. Pour the sauce over the chops and serve immediately.

QUICK n' PAINLESS

To make this dish even faster, use dried apples, which you don't have to peel or chop. Add 1/2 cup of dried apple rings or slices to the skillet in step 3. The heat and liquid will soften them, although they'll retain an agreeably chewy texture. Dried apples will add a much more intense apple flavor to the dish—you may find that you pre-fer them to fresh.

Mock Baked Ham with Mustard Glaze

In the interest of flavor, canned picnic hams can be baked, their surfaces glazed and scored with a diamond pattern. It's not because they're raw—they come fully cooked—but because it tastes better to heat the ham through and glaze it. You can achieve that same flavor, however, in a few minutes on top of the stove, by heating the ham slices in a sauce until it reduces to a glaze.

To serve 4, use a thick slice off a whole large canned picnic ham (the kind made famous by David Letterman who tosses them to the audience), or buy one of those thick ham steaks, 1¹/₂ to 2 pounds, which come in vacuum packs. Serve with mashed potatoes and green peas.

Serves 4

³/₄ cup orange juice or pineapple juice

1 tablespoon Dijon mustard

1 tablespoon brown sugar

4 whole cloves (optional)

One 2-pound slab of cooked ham (preferably canned picnic ham or vacuum-packed ham steak)

1　In a large skillet, combine the juice, mustard, brown sugar, and cloves, if using. Heat over medium heat until the liquid starts to bubble.

2　Add the ham to the skillet and turn it over so both sides are coated. Cook for 6 to 8 minutes, turning once or twice, until the glaze reduces and coats the ham, and the ham is heated through.

QUICK n' PAINLESS

Leftover ham is great for sandwiches, but you can get a super-quick hot meal out of it by cubing any leftovers and adding them to a cooked package of macaroni and cheese. You can also heat cubed ham with a can of baked beans, and doll it up with a squirt of ketchup, a big spoonful of spicy brown mustard, and a small spoonful of molasses. It's also a tasty addition to the Kielbasa "Cassoulet" that follows, if you don't mind doubling up on pork products.

Quick Pork Curry with Cauliflower

Cauliflower may seem like an odd choice to add to a meat curry, although it's often curried with potatoes or other vegetables in Indian cuisine. Added to a meat curry, though, it soaks up the flavor, and cooks down to a delicious consistency, helping to thicken the sauce. Best of all for the busy cook, you have the meat and the vegetable in one pot, and you only need to cook some rice to go with it.

This recipe is a perfect reason to keep a jar of curry paste in your pantry. It has a much more developed and authentic flavor than most commercially available curry powders.

Serves 4

2 medium onions

3 tablespoons vegetable oil

4 to 6 cloves garlic

1 pound pork cubes

$^1/_4$ cup curry paste

1 head cauliflower

3 cups water

1 beef or chicken stock cube

2 tablespoons tomato paste

1 Chop the onions coarsely (you can do this quickly in the food processor).

2 Heat the oil in a large heavy saucepan or stew pot over medium heat. Add the chopped onions and pass the garlic cloves through a garlic press directly into the pan. Cook 3 minutes, until the onions soften and brown slightly.

QUICK n' PAINLESS

For speed, buy the cubes of pork marked "stew" in the meat section of your supermarket. Or ask the butcher to cube some shoulder or butt meat for you.

3 Add the pork cubes and brown, stirring occasionally, for 3 minutes. Stir in the curry paste.

4 Break the cauliflower into florets directly into the pot. Add the water, stock cube, and tomato paste and stir the pot well. Raise the heat and bring it to a boil.

5 Cover loosely, lower the heat slightly, and cook at a low boil for about 20 minutes, stirring occasionally to make sure it doesn't stick to the bottom. After 20 minutes, the sauce should be thickened, the pork tender, and the cauliflower will have broken into small pieces. Serve with white rice.

IF YOU'RE SO INCLINED

You can make this same curry with beef or lamb, but the cooking time should be extended by about 15 minutes for the meat to be tender. You can also substitute eggplant cubes (with the skin on) for the cauliflower, and use different varieties and heat levels of curry pastes. This one basic recipe can turn into dozens of curries!

Kielbasa "Cassoulet"

Real cassoulet is an elaborate dish from the South of France made of beans and many meats, including garlicky sausage, that can take months to make when you take into account the preparation of the preserved duck or goose that goes into it. Despite the name, I'm not pretending this is cassoulet by any means, but it was inspired by that dish, and there's a good hint of it in the garlicky kielbasa and white beans, as well as in the traditional bread-crumb crust. Best of all, it takes less than half an hour, with only about 5 minutes of preparation time.

Serves 4

One (1 pound) ring of kielbasa

Two (16 ounce) cans navy beans (or other white bean such as cannellini)

3 tablespoons tomato paste

1 tablespoon molasses

1 teaspoon dried thyme

1 teaspoon salt

Freshly ground black pepper

1 cup bread crumbs

2 tablespoons olive oil

1. Preheat oven to 375°. Slice the kielbasa into 1/4- to 1/2-inch rounds and place in a 2-quart casserole.

2. Add the beans and their liquid, and then add the tomato paste, molasses, thyme, salt, and a few grindings of black pepper. Stir well to combine.

3 Sprinkle the bread crumbs over the whole dish, and dash on a little more salt and pepper. Drizzle with the olive oil.

4 Bake for 20 to 25 minutes, until the casserole is bubbling and the bread crumbs are browned but not burned.

Like real cassoulet, this is a hearty and filling dish, best saved for a cold night. Lower the lights, grab a crusty baguette, and pour yourself a nice glass of red wine. Snuggle under a warm blanket and enjoy your South of France delicacy (for two perhaps?).

The Lazy Way

Getting Time on Your Side

	The Old Way	The Lazy Way
Whipping up a tempting Russian Stroganoff	1½ hours	15 minutes
Making a classic Indian curry	2 hours	30 minute
Preparing a dish of French cassoulet	3 months	30 minutes
Baking a ham with a mustard glaze	1 hour	7 minutes
Slicing beef for fajitas	15 minutes	0 minutes
Preparing a standing rib roast for an elaborate dinner party	3½ hours (c'mon! that's not a dish for the busy kitchen!)	0 hours

Chicken on the Run: Clucking Good Chicken Recipes

Boneless chicken breasts are your best bet for quick-cooking poultry. They can be a little pricey compared to buying the whole bird (especially if you buy even more expensive cuts, such as breast pieces trimmed into strips or nuggets), but the time savings are well worth it. Without bones and skin it will only take you a few extra seconds to trim the breasts into even faster-cooking strips and cubes.

A whole chicken cut into pieces will cook in less than half an hour in the oven, but if you have a little extra time, a whole roasted chicken is a surprisingly easy alternative, because you don't have to cut it up or handle it excessively. You can sprinkle a few seasonings on the outside, cook it at quite a high heat for speed, and have a moist and delicious roast bird ready in an hour. You may even end up with some leftovers for sandwiches or chicken salad. Roasting vegetables in the pan with chicken sounds like a good idea, but it will actually slow your cooking time and saturate the vegetables with grease. If you don't have any extra time, and may be watching the calories, instead, set baking potatoes on an upper oven rack while the chicken cooks and cook some broccoli or carrots on top of the stove.

Rotisserie chickens, either from one of several national chains or from the deli section of your supermarket, are a blessing to cooks on the run. The intense heat and slow cooking of the rotisserie process makes the chicken deliciously browned on the outside, and they're usually very moist on the inside. Buy a large one and serve it carved, as if it was a regular roast chicken you just pulled out of the oven, or get a smaller one and strip off the meat to incorporate into salads, sandwiches, and casseroles.

Chicken Cacciatorini

I call my version of the Italian chicken stew Cacciatorini, or "Little Cacciatori," because it hints at the classic slow-cooked flavors but in a zippy 20-minute kind of way.

Serves 4

4 boneless, skinless chicken breasts

1 green or red pepper

1 small yellow onion

2 tablespoons olive oil

2 cloves garlic

One 15-ounce can chopped tomatoes

1 teaspoon dried oregano

1 teaspoon dried basil

Salt and pepper

Parmesan cheese

1 Cut the chicken breasts in half lengthwise. Use the food processor to cut the pepper and onion into a medium dice.

2 In a large nonstick skillet, heat the olive oil over medium-high heat and sauté the chicken breasts for about 3 minutes on each side, until browned.

3 Add the pepper, onion, and garlic and sauté 3 to 4 minutes until the vegetables start to soften.

4 Add the tomatoes (in the juice), oregano, and basil. Cover and simmer gently for 10 to 12 minutes until the pepper and onion are soft but not mushy, and the sauce starts to thicken somewhat. Season with salt and lots of black pepper, and serve with Parmesan cheese over pasta.

QUICK n' PAINLESS

For an even faster version of this dish, sauté the chicken breasts in olive oil and then pour a pint jar of your favorite pasta sauce over them and heat through. If you use a good-quality pasta sauce (one without added sugar) flavored with peppers and onions, you'll come even closer to approximating the flavor.

Crispy Chicken Breasts with Fresh Tomato Sauce

This method for quick-cooking deliciously crispy chicken breasts will become a standby. Eat them alone with a squeeze of lemon juice or any sauce, or with the Fresh Tomato Sauce offered here.

The addition of cornmeal gives the cooked chicken breasts a crispy bite and helps the chicken brown and look more appetizing. If you don't have cornmeal on hand, you can use flour alone.

Serves 2

For chicken

2 skinless, boneless chicken breasts

1 tablespoon cornmeal

1 tablespoon all-purpose flour

$1/2$ teaspoon salt

$1/4$ teaspoon black pepper

Pinch of paprika

2 to 3 tablespoons vegetable oil or olive oil

For sauce

1 medium ripe tomato (preferably a juicy beefsteak tomato)

$1/2$ lemon

$1/2$ clove garlic

$1/2$ teaspoon salt

$1/4$ teaspoon black pepper

2 tablespoons extra-virgin olive oil

YOU'LL THANK YOURSELF LATER

Cook a couple of extra chicken breasts and store them in the refrigerator. Slice them on the diagonal during the week for sandwiches, either for a quick supper (with a bowl of soup) or for an easy brown-bag lunch.

1 Flatten the chicken breasts with the heel of your hand (or give them a few whacks with a meat pounder).

2 To make the chicken, combine the cornmeal, flour, salt, pepper, and paprika on a plate. Roll the chicken in the mixture, pressing to coat.

3 In a large skillet, heat the oil over medium-high heat. Put the chicken in the pan and cook it for about 5 minutes on each side, until it's golden brown and cooked through. Remove to a serving plate.

4 While the chicken is cooking, cut the core out of the tomato and cut it into chunks. Toss the tomato into the blender.

5 Squeeze the lemon juice directly into the blender, catching the seeds in a strainer or with your hand. Add the garlic, salt, pepper, and olive oil. Blend until smooth and creamy. Pour over the cooked chicken and serve. If you let this sauce sit for too long, it may start to separate, but it will recombine easily with a few pulses of the blender.

IF YOU'RE SO
INCLINED

The fresh tomato sauce, made by whipping raw tomato with olive oil to make a delicious emulsion, is a terrifically versatile sauce that's wonderful with many dishes besides chicken. Spoon it over fish or grilled or steamed vegetables or dollop some on top of toasted cheese sandwiches.

Quickest Cashew Chicken

This entree cooks so quickly that you must remember to put your rice on before starting the chicken, or you'll find you've gotten too far ahead of yourself. Broccoli makes a good accompaniment.

Serves 2 to 3

1 pound (2 to 3) boneless, skinless chicken breasts

1 medium yellow onion

3 scallions

2 cloves garlic

1 teaspoon cornstarch

2 tablespoons water

2 tablespoons cooking oil

1 tablespoon soy sauce

1 tablespoon lemon juice or cider vinegar

1/4 cup salted cashews

1 Cut the chicken breasts into narrow strips. Peel the onions and coarsely chop into large chunks.

2 Cut the green tops of the scallions into 1-inch pieces, cutting the whites somewhat more finely. Mince the garlic. Mix the cornstarch with the water and set aside.

3 In a large nonstick skillet, heat the oil over high heat. Add the onions, stir-fry for 2 to 3 minutes, add the scallions and garlic, and stir-fry for another 1 to 2 minutes.

4 Keeping the heat high, add the chicken strips and cook 3 to 4 minutes until the chicken is opaque.

5 Stir in the soy sauce, lemon juice, and cashews; and then pour the cornstarch mixture over all and toss for a minute or two. Serve immediately over rice.

Baked Chicken with Lemon and Herbs

Although this dish takes longer to cook than most of the other recipes in this chapter, the preparation time is next to nothing. A whole jointed chicken, or pieces such as thighs or drumsticks, are slapped into a casserole dish and covered with a few seasonings in about 2 minutes. The whole thing is then baked until it's succulent and fragrant. You can even lay the chicken in the dish in the morning, add the seasonings, and leave it marinating in the fridge all day. Then pop the pan into the oven when you come home.

Serves 4 to 6

$^1/_4$ cup olive oil

3 pounds chicken pieces (a whole jointed chicken or thighs, drumsticks, etc.)

1 lemon

8 to 10 cloves garlic (left unpeeled)

1 teaspoon dried thyme or rosemary

Salt and pepper

1 Preheat the oven to 350°. Pour the olive oil into a 9 × 13" baking dish. Add the chicken pieces and turn them so they're coated with oil.

2 Squeeze the lemon over the chicken. Scatter the unpeeled garlic cloves in the pan and sprinkle the chicken pieces with thyme or rosemary. Season well with salt and pepper.

3 Bake for 30 to 35 minutes until tender and cooked through.

IF YOU'RE SO INCLINED

You can vary the flavor of this dish by following the recipe but substituting lime juice for lemon and cumin for the thyme or rosemary. Sprinkle some red chili flakes over the prepared pieces before putting the pan in the oven for added zip.

Chicken Thighs with Cucumber Raita

Chicken thighs are dark meat. Though moister and often more flavorful than breast meat, they take longer to cook through to the bone. More and more supermarkets are starting to carry boned chicken thighs, though, so if you see them, snap them up. Skin them to cut down on fat and to speed up cooking, and trim them so they open out horizontally to thin them. Sautéed with a little curry flavoring and served with the raita, which is a cooling cucumber sauce, and accompanied by rice and green peas, it's a perfect summer meal.

Serves 4

For chicken

4 large boneless chicken thighs (or 8 small ones)

2 tablespoons curry paste

2 tablespoons cooking oil

1/4 cup chicken stock or water

For raita

1 medium cucumber

1 small onion

1 fresh green chili, such as a jalapeño or serrano (optional)

1/2 teaspoon salt

1/4 teaspoon cumin

1/2 cup plain yogurt

1. Skin the chicken thighs and cut in half horizontally. Smear them on both sides with the curry paste.

2. In a large nonstick skillet, heat the oil over medium-high heat. Sauté the chicken thighs for about 5 minutes on each side until browned.

3. Add chicken stock or water, lower the heat, and cover. Let cook for 5 minutes while you make the raita.

4. Peel the cucumber and onion, cut them into 3 to 4 chunks, and drop them into the food processor.

5. Cut the top and tail off the fresh chili and cut in half. Remove the seeds, if desired, or leave them in for extra heat. Add the chili to the processor bowl.

6. Add the salt, cumin, and yogurt. Pulse briefly until you have a coarsely combined, chunky mixture. Do not puree into a mush.

7. Place one thigh on each plate and spoon a mound of the sauce next to it.

IF YOU'RE SO INCLINED

To make the cucumber raita into even more of a salad, add a fresh plum tomato. Cut out the core of a small ripe tomato, cut the tomato in half horizontally, and lightly squeeze out the juice and seeds into the sink (or garbage) before adding the tomato flesh to the food processor.

Sesame-Soy Roast Chicken

There are endless things you can do to a chicken to season it before roasting, but the simpler, the better. You can simply salt and pepper the bird and pop it in the oven, but the skin will be tastier if you add a touch more flavoring. The recipe below relies on aromatic toasted sesame oil, which gives the skin a delectable flavor. The soy sauce helps the skin achieve that yummy-looking mahogany color and replaces the salt.

To make this chicken really fast, roast a smallish bird, about 3 pounds, and follow the high heat roasting technique described.

Serves 4

One 2$\frac{1}{2}$- to 3-pound whole chicken
2 tablespoons dark sesame oil
2 tablespoons soy sauce
Freshly ground black pepper

1 Preheat the oven to 400°. Line a roasting pan with foil.

2 Rinse the bird inside and out under cool running water and pat dry with a paper towel. Smooth the sesame oil and soy sauce all over the outside of the bird, using your hands.

3 Lay the chicken in the roasting pan breast side down, so that the fattier juices of the back drip through the breast while roasting. Grind some black pepper over the bird.

4 Roast for about 1 hour. The chicken is done when the legs move easily and the juices run clear when the thigh is pierced with the tip of a knife. If the juices are rosy or tinged with pink, return to the oven for another 10 to 15 minutes.

Chicken-Noodle Casserole

I'm not a big fan of cooking with cans of high-sodium cream soups, but such dishes certainly have their place in American cuisine and also in my own kitchen. I'm quite fond of this chicken version of the classic tuna casserole, made with macaroni and a can of green beans (substitute corn or peas, if you like). I've turned to it on more than one busy night.

Serves 4 to 6

- 1 pound macaroni
- 2 to 3 cups cooked chicken meat (from 1 small rotisserie chicken)
- 1 can cream of mushroom soup
- 1 cup milk
- 1 can green beans, peas, or corn

1   Cook macaroni according to package directions. (While the macaroni cooks, strip the meat off the bones of the chicken and cut the meat into bite-sized pieces.)

2   In a large saucepan, stir the soup and milk until the mixture is smooth. Drain the vegetable and add to the soup mixture along with the chicken. Heat over medium heat.

3   Drain the macaroni and add the hot pasta to the mixture. Stir gently and heat through before serving.

IF YOU'RE SO
INCLINED

If you have the time, turn the chicken and macaroni mixture into a casserole dish, and top it with some grated cheese, buttered bread crumbs, or crumbled bacon (that's been cooked in the microwave). Bake at 350° for 20 minutes or so, until the casserole is bubbling.

I'm not squeamish about caressing naked chicken; but when I'm in a hurry, I wear my rubber work gloves because then I don't have to stop and wipe or rinse my hands between steps. Put the gloves on to rinse the bird. Lay it in the pan and slip off one glove to take off the lids and pour on the sesame oil and soy sauce. Slide your glove back on and rub the oil and soy all over the bird with both hands. Take off the gloves to grind on pepper, open the oven, and set the pan in. Slip the gloves on and rinse them with soap and hot water. The whole job takes about 2 hassle-free minutes, and you don't have grease and raw chicken juices on your hands.

Middle Eastern Chicken and Rice Salad

Generally, if you buy an already cooked rotisserie chicken, you don't want to do anything more than carve and eat it. But when you want something a little different, rotisserie chickens are ideal for any dish that requires cooked chicken, particularly chicken salads and casseroles.

Strip the meat off the bones, coarsely chop (or use scissors to cut) very large pieces such as the breasts, and proceed with any recipe calling for cooked chicken, such as this Middle Eastern-inspired chicken pasta salad—a whole meal in a bowl. The turmeric gives the salad its distinctive and lovely yellow color.

Serves 4

1^1/2 cups raw rice

1 lemon

1 clove garlic

^{3}/4 cup plain yogurt

1 teaspoon turmeric (or curry powder, if desired)

^{1}/4 to ^{1}/2 cup chopped fresh parsley

1 teaspoon salt

Black pepper

One 8-ounce jar artichoke hearts

2 cups cooked chicken meat (from 1 small rotisserie chicken)

^{1}/4 cup raisins

Slivered toasted almonds (optional, for garnish)

1 In a medium saucepan, cook the rice with 3 cups of water, according to package directions.

2 While the rice cooks, make the dressing in the bottom of a large mixing bowl. Juice the lemon and pass the garlic through a garlic press directly into the bowl. Add the yogurt, turmeric, parsley, salt, and pepper, and stir.

3 Drain and coarsely chop the artichokes and let them marinate in the dressing while you finish the rest of the salad.

4 When the rice is cooked, rinse it in cold water to quickly cool it, and drain it in a colander. Add the cold, drained rice to the dressing and artichokes in the large mixing bowl, along with the chicken and raisins. Toss gently to combine.

5 Garnish with almonds, if desired, and serve. This dish keeps well for one night if tightly covered.

YOU'LL THANK YOURSELF LATER

When you make the rice, add an extra cupful (and 2 extra cupsful of water) to the pot to make extra rice for a quick meal later of fried rice. Store the extra rice in the refrigerator—fried rice must be made with leftover cold rice or it will be sticky.

The peaches don't have to be peeled for this curry, but if you have a real aversion to their fuzzy skin, drop them in boiling water for 1 minute, then drain and rinse under cold water. The skins will slip right off. Or be sure to use nectarines instead, whose smooth skins don't require peeling. You can also substitute 6 ripe apricots or 2 ripe, but not mushy, mangos in place of the fruit in this recipe.

Chicken and Fruit Curry on the Run

This recipe is a particular favorite of mine. Though curries starting with raw meat have a much more intense flavor, the addition of fruit makes this milder, with more than a hint of sweet and sour in the balance between the fruit and the lemon juice. It only takes about 10 minutes of cooking time to make a curry sauce before you add the chicken meat, stripped off a rotisserie chicken, and the sliced fruit. Make sure to start cooking the rice before you put on the curry so everything will be ready at once. A spicy fruit chutney or Indian lime pickle is a good accompaniment.

Serves 4 to 6

2 medium onions

3 tablespoons vegetable oil

2 cloves garlic

1/4 cup curry paste (preferably a medium-heat paste)

2 cups water

1 chicken stock cube

2 tablespoons tomato paste

3 medium nectarines or peaches, perfectly ripe

2 1/2 to 3 cups cooked chicken (from 1 medium rotisserie chicken)

1 Chop the onions (in the food processor if you like). In a large saucepan, heat the vegetable oil over medium heat and add the onions.

2 Pass the garlic through a garlic press directly into the pan. Sauté for 3 to 4 minutes, until the onion is softened.

3 Stir in the curry paste and cook for 2 minutes, stirring so it doesn't stick (this step brings out the flavor of the spices). Pour in the water, and add the stock cube and tomato paste.

4 Bring to a boil, lower the heat, and simmer the sauce for about 10 minutes, until it starts to thicken. While the sauce is boiling, cut the nectarines or peaches into slices and discard the pits (it's also a good time to strip the meat off the chicken, if you haven't done so already).

5 Add the chicken and fruit to the curry sauce, reduce the heat, and simmer very gently for 7 to 8 minutes, to heat through and combine the flavors. Serve over hot white rice.

QUICK 🆚 PAINLESS

Use canned peaches to make this dish even faster. Ideally, buy the kind packed in concentrated fruit juice, not heavy syrup, but if all you have on hand is the syrupy kind, drain and rinse them under cold running water.

Getting Time on Your Side

	The Old Way	The Lazy Way
Concocting an elegant sauce to top your sautéed chicken breasts	20 minutes	2 minutes
Roasting a whole chicken	2½ hours	1 hour
Stewing up a Chicken Cacciatore	2 to 3 hours	20 minutes
Making a chicken salad	2 hours	15 minutes
Preparing a flavorful chicken curry	2 hours	25 minutes
Figuring out what to put on the kids' sandwiches in the morning	10 minutes	0 minutes (leftover chicken!)

Chapter
eleven

Flying Fish

Seafood, from fish fillets to shellfish, is a fast-cooking dream, but it has the drawback of not keeping fresh for very long. So, although fresh fish and shellfish are tasty and healthy, you have to plan in advance a bit more than you do for beef or chicken, which sit quietly in the fridge for several days longer. The safest and most hassle-free option for busy cooks is to buy frozen seafood, or to store your fresh seafood in the freezer, unless you're cooking it the same day you bought it.

In the case of thin fillets, you can cook them straight from the freezer, which makes freezing quite a practical storage option. Put sheets of waxed paper between the fillets before freezing and you can pull out one or two instead of a whole block.

Fish is not only fast-cooking, but eating it at least twice a week is great for your heart (and possibly your brain, too). Increase the amount of fish in your diet by keeping a selection of "gourmet" fillets in the freezer, such as salmon steaks, orange roughy, lemon sole, or mahi mahi.

Packages of frozen fish resemble bricks when frozen, but they're a terrific main course for the busy cook to keep on hand in the freezer. It takes about 5 minutes to defrost blocks of fillets in the microwave, or you can place a block, still wrapped, in a bowl of cold water on the counter before you go to work, and you'll have thawed fillets to pry apart and sauté when you get home that evening. Wrap extras in plastic wrap and store a day or two over ice in the refrigerator, but never refreeze.

Pan-Fried Fish Fillets with Quick Curry Sauce

Here is a basic recipe that's the quickest way to sauté and have white fish on the table with the most flavor possible. Broiling fish is also an excellent method for a busy night (just be sure you line the broiler pan with foil first for easy cleanup), but sautéing gives you the option of making a delicious sauce in the nonstick skillet in seconds—just the thing to coax any reluctant fish eaters you might have around the table.

Sautéing gives the fish a nice brown finish and crispy edge. You can eat it plain, with a squeeze of lemon and a little butter if you like. Or try this easy curry sauce, which gives a Southern Indian flavor to the dish (make sure you only use unsweetened coconut milk, not the kind for piña coladas). It gives the fish a rich exotic flavor with very little fuss. Serve with rice and a green salad.

Serves 4

For the fish

4 fish fillets, fresh or frozen (try cod, plaice, whitefish, flounder, sole, whiting, or any flat white fish)

Flour

Salt and pepper

2 tablespoons butter

For curry sauce

1 medium onion

2 teaspoons curry powder or paste

One 15-ounce can coconut milk

1. Rinse the fish and pat dry. Place some flour on a plate and roll the fish in it, patting to make the flour cling. Season with salt and pepper.

2. In a large skillet, heat the butter over medium heat. Add the fish and cook for about 5 minutes, turning it halfway through. You can serve the fish immediately or place it on a warm dish on the back of the stove while you make the curry sauce.

3. For curry sauce, finely dice the onion, add to the hot pan, and sauté until the onion starts to brown. Stir in the curry powder or paste. Pour in the coconut milk and bring it to a boil.

4. Simmer for 4 to 5 minutes until the sauce starts to thicken slightly. Return the fish to the pan and heat through. Serve immediately.

IF YOU'RE SO
INCLINED

If you can find authentic Indian naan bread, heat it in the oven and serve on the side. It's similar to a big soft pita, but if you can't find it, heat some white pitas in the oven until warm and soft, but not toasted or crisp. Dip them in the curry sauce as you eat.

A COMPLETE WASTE OF TIME

The 3 Worst Things to Do with Fish Fillets:

1. Turn them too often (more than once) when sautéing or broiling them, which makes them break apart and more inclined to dry out.

2. Store fresh fish in the refrigerator without putting it in a bowl of ice, which keeps it fresh and stops it from picking up other flavors or odors.

3. Cook them until they fall apart or dry out.

Baked Salmon with Mustard-Dill Sauce

The Scandinavians have long known that a piquant dill sauce brings out the best in salmon's delicately oily orange flesh. Buy the freshest fish available; if it's well-wrapped, it can be kept in the coldest part of the fridge for three days at the most.

To store without freezing, place the wrapped fish on a bowl of ice in the fridge, and remember that sooner rather than later should be your rule of thumb when it comes to fresh fish. Buy steaks no thicker than 1½ inches, which will cook through quickly. This recipe also works very well with any white fish fillets.

Serves 4

4 salmon steaks
Salt and pepper
½ cup light cream
1½ tablespoons Dijon mustard
1 tablespoon fresh (or 1 teaspoon dried) dill weed

1 Preheat the oven to 350°. Lightly coat a medium casserole with cooking spray and arrange the fish in the pan. Season with salt and pepper.

2 In a small bowl, mix together cream, mustard, and dill, and pour over the top of the fish.

3 Bake for 20 minutes until the sauce is bubbling lightly and the fish is opaque.

Fish Fillets en Papillote

"En papillote" is the French term for food cooked in little parchment paper or foil packages. Although parchment paper makes a lovely looking package, aluminum foil makes a tighter and more reliable seal for busy cooks.

Serves 4

4 fish fillets (try anything: salmon, shark, any white fish, mackerel, etc.)

Butter or olive oil

Herbs, fresh or dried (try oregano, dill, rosemary, parsley, thyme)

1 lemon

Salt and pepper

1 medium zucchini or carrot (optional)

1　Preheat the oven to 350°. Lay four 12-inch squares of aluminum foil or parchment paper on a baking sheet.

2　Place a fillet of fish on each square, dot with butter or drizzle with olive oil, and add a few sprigs or sprinkles of herbs, as desired.

3　Slice the lemon thinly and distribute the rings among the packets. Season well with salt and pepper.

4　If using zucchini or other vegetables, grate them in a food processor and distribute them among the packets.

5　Fold the packages in half and twist the edges together to seal. Bake for 20 to 25 minutes until the packages are puffed up with steam. Serve individual packets on each plate and tear them open with forks.

YOU'LL THANK YOURSELF LATER

Make a few extra fish fillets en papillote and don't cook them. Fold the edges tightly to seal, and freeze them in a plastic bag to prevent freezer burn. If you have different ingredients in each packet, put the various types in different plastic bags, and label the bags with masking tape. On busy nights, put as many as you need on a baking sheet, straight from the freezer, and bake for 25 to 30 minutes. Et voilà!

Individually frozen (preferably uncooked) shrimp are excellent to keep in the freezer, not only for a quick dinner but also to add to stir-fried rice or to stir into a cream soup as a garnish.

Zesty Fiesta Shrimp

It's not hard to find something to do with shrimp when it comes your way, and it's best to do very little with it to let the sweet flavor of the shellfish shine. For fresh shrimp, go lightly on the garlic and red chili, adding just a hint to enliven the seafood. If you use frozen shrimp, however, a little extra butter, chili flakes, and lemon juice help mask the fact that the shrimp aren't fresh. If you buy the shrimp already shelled and deveined, you won't have to bother with that step yourself.

Do not thaw frozen shrimp before cooking. The heat of the pan will thaw and cook them through in about a minute or two. Because this dish cooks so quickly, have the rest of your meal ready to serve before you start cooking the shrimp.

The scallions are optional, but they serve to bulk up the dish and help make a nice sauce. Serve over rice, with a green salad and plenty of bread to sop up the fragrant juices.

Serves 4

4 cloves garlic

2 to 3 scallions (optional)

2 tablespoons extra-virgin olive oil

2 tablespoons butter

1/4 to 1/2 teaspoon dried red chili flakes

1 pound medium to large shrimp, fresh or frozen, shelled and deveined

1/2 lemon

1 Mince the garlic or put it through a garlic press. Coarsely chop the scallions if using and set aside.

2. In a large skillet, heat the olive oil and butter over medium heat. As the foam of the butter subsides, add the garlic and red chili flakes, and sauté for about 1 minute until the garlic smells pungent. Be very careful not to burn it, or you'll ruin the whole dish.

3. Turn up the heat slightly and add the shrimp and chopped scallions if desired. Sauté for 2 to 3 minutes until the shrimp is opaque and cooked through.

4. Squeeze the juice of 1/2 lemon over the whole dish and serve immediately.

Congratulations! You're eating a lot more fish and you probably feel better for it. Put on an old sweatshirt and use all that newfound energy to go toss a football around the front yard with your spouse or kids or friends on a sunny fall afternoon. Dinner can wait—after all, it'll only take you a few minutes to sauté some fish!

The Lazy Way

Stir-Fried Shrimp with Snow Peas

Shrimp makes stir-frying even faster than it already is, especially when you buy it already shelled and deveined. When combined with a quick-cooking, tender green vegetable such as snow peas (or fresh spinach leaves), you can have a beautiful meal ready in about 10 minutes (provided your rice is cooked, which takes about 15 minutes, so start it before you prepare the stir-fry ingredients).

Stir-frying is one of the fastest ways in and out of the kitchen—if you buy ready-cleaned raw shrimp (fresh is best, but frozen will do), you can have this dish on the table before a Chinese restaurant would have time to deliver.

Serves 4

2 cups snow peas

2 scallions

One 1-inch piece of fresh ginger

1 clove garlic

1 teaspoon cornstarch

2 tablespoons water

1 tablespoon cooking oil

1 pound large raw shrimp, fresh or frozen, shelled and deveined

$1/4$ cup chicken stock or water

2 tablespoons soy sauce

1 Rinse and drain the snow peas and cut the scallions into 1-inch pieces. Grate the fresh ginger with a mini-food processor or grater, and mince the garlic.

2 In a small cup, mix the cornstarch with 2 tablespoons of water and set aside.

3 In a large nonstick skillet, heat the oil over high heat. Add the garlic and ginger, stir-fry for about 30 seconds, add the scallions, and cook for 1 minute.

4 Add shrimp and stir-fry for 1 minute. Add snow peas, stock or water, and soy sauce. Cook for 1 to 2 minutes until the peas are bright green and the shrimp is opaque.

5 Stir in the cornstarch mixture, toss well, and serve immediately.

IF YOU'RE SO
INCLINED

Sometimes food just tastes better when you create the right atmosphere. Set the table with chopsticks and serve green tea with dinner. If you can find some, end the meal with fortune cookies and have everyone read theirs aloud.

Fish Cakes with Lime Butter

These tasty little cakes can be thrown together in minutes and cooked right away or left to chill in the refrigerator all day or overnight. When you're ready to eat, just pat on the sesame seeds and fry. The lime butter is a quick and zesty sauce, but the cakes are just as good plain, or with a dollop of tartar sauce.

I usually use canned salmon, but you can also use leftover cooked white fish (or even microwave a package of whitefish fillets just for the purpose). Serve on a bed of crisp lettuce with a green vegetable such as peas or asparagus. If you don't have sesame seeds to coat the outsides of the fish cakes, substitute bread crumbs, crushed corn flakes, or flour.

QUICK n' PAINLESS

Instead of frying, you can bake these cakes, which will save you effort though not time. Preheat the oven to 350°. Spray-grease a baking sheet and place the sesame seed-coated cakes on it. Spray a thin layer of the spray oil over their surfaces, to help brown, and bake them for 30 to 35 minutes, until heated through and lightly browned on the outside.

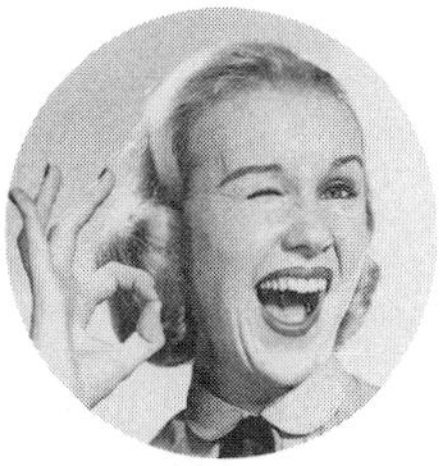

Serves 4

- 1 onion
- 3 slices stale bread, white or brown
- One (15-ounce) can salmon (or a scant 2 cups cooked whitefish)
- 1 large egg
- 1 tablespoon dried parsley
- 1 1/2 teaspoons salt
- Black pepper
- Cooking oil
- 1/4 cup sesame seeds (or bread crumbs, crushed corn flakes, or flour)
- 1/4 cup (1/2 stick) butter
- 1 lime

1. Chop the onion in the food processor. Add the stale bread and pulse until it forms coarse crumbs.

2. Drain the fish if you use canned salmon. Add the fish, egg, parsley, salt, and pepper to the food processor and pulse.

3. In a skillet, heat about 1/2 inch of cooking oil over medium-high heat.

4. Form the mixture into 8 small, roundish patties or 4 large, flatter ones. Roll each patty lightly in sesame seeds (or dust with flour) and fry in oil until golden, about 5 minutes on each side. The oil should be quite hot, or else the fish cakes will soak up too much of it.

5. Place the butter in a cup and microwave it for less than a minute until it is just melted and not bubbling. Squeeze the lime juice into the melted butter, whisk quickly with a fork, and serve with the fish cakes.

YOU'LL THANK YOURSELF LATER

You can form these fish cakes, coat with sesame seeds or bread crumbs, and freeze them with a layer of waxed paper in between each in a zipperlock plastic bag (lay the cakes flat in the freezer until they're frozen solid. Lift out as many cakes as you need and fry or bake them directly from the freezer (adding a few extra minutes of cooking time to heat them through). If you make the cakes into small balls or patties, you can serve them with a dollop of tartar sauce as an appetizer or starter.

The 3 Worst Things to Do with Fresh Scallops:

1. **Buy tiny flavorless bay scallops instead of big moist sea scallops.**

2. **Overseason so that the sweet taste of the seafood can't shine through.**

3. **Let them sit too long before serving so they have time to cool and toughen.**

Scallops in White Wine

Shellfish is a great treat for anyone, but its super fast-cooking qualities and the easy professional finish you can achieve with it make it particularly useful for the lazy kitchen. Have the rest of the meal ready to go before you start cooking the scallops. Try serving them with noodles, a substantial, well-dressed green salad, and crusty bread to soak up the juices.

Serves 4

1 pound large, fresh sea scallops
3 tablespoons butter
1/4 cup white wine
Salt and pepper

1 Drain the liquid from the scallops. In a large nonstick skillet, heat the butter over medium high heat until it's sizzling but not browned.

2 Add the scallops and sauté, keeping the heat up, for 2 to 3 minutes until the scallops are white and cooked through, with a hint of browning at the edges.

3 Pour over the wine and bring to a very quick boil. Sprinkle on salt and pepper and serve immediately.

Getting Time on Your Side

	The Old Way	**The Lazy Way**
Putting a protein on the dinner plate	1 1/2 hours (roast beef)	10 minutes (sautéed fish)
Defrosting fish fillets before cooking	4 to 5 hours	5 minutes
Cleaning and deveining shrimp	25 minutes	0 minutes (buy them cleaned)
Finely chopping ginger and garlic for stir-frying	6 minutes	1 minute
Melting butter for a sauce	5 minutes (stovetop)	30 seconds (microwave)
Coaxing the kids to eat fish	30 minutes (boiled cod)	0 minutes (fish cakes!)

Just Throw It All In: One-Dish Meals

In this chapter, a "one-dish meal" means one finished product that comprises the entire meal—protein, carbohydrate, and vegetables—and that almost always involves only one pot. Even when there's an extra step involved, such as cooking the pasta or microwaving the spinach, the busy cook still tends to come out ahead in terms of labor saved.

The slow cooker is an obvious place to start, and the lazy kitchen shouldn't be without one, even if it's used only to cook dried beans. For stews, a slow cooker can be a little less effective than stovetop cooking because the meat doesn't brown unless you brown it first on top of the stove (in that case, if I've already started cooking, I'd just as soon finish cooking the dish myself). Irish stew is the exception, and slow cookers were made for it. The lamb chops take on a tender, unctuous quality, the vegetables slowly cook down into their own sauce, and coming home to a finished pot of stew after a day at the office is as warming and hearty as a turf fire.

And then there's always pizza—not the delivery kind, but a quick and easy kind you can make at home. They have far less fat and far more nutrition than the grease-laden pies that arrive at your door, which makes these pita pizzas much more practical (cheaper as well!) for a regular weeknight supper.

Other options include stove-top pasta and rice dishes with sausage, fish, or chicken, and yes, the occasional can of condensed soup as a sauce. I don't like to use canned soup in my cooking very often, but now and then it's okay to use canned soup, and other canned foods, such as vegetables, for the fastest, easiest route to a hot meal. Frozen green peas, corn, and spinach in particular make great vegetable additions to one-pot dishes, providing taste, color, texture, and nutrition.

You'll find less emphasis on cooking with really fresh ingredients in this chapter, but all-in-one meals are for those cooks who need to get something on the table without a lot of effort after a tiring day at work. And that may mean combining several cans of something. Some of the dishes below, such as the Chicken Pot Pie, are among the most comforting of comfort food—and if a can of soup can help provide that, so much the better!

Salmon Noodle Casserole with Peas

If you're anything like me, tuna casserole is one of your old standbys. I've made and eaten my share, always with that faint embarrassment that I wouldn't necessarily want anyone to catch me eating it, but that, my goodness, it actually does taste pretty good, doesn't it? Lest anyone catch me, I've started stocking a can or two of salmon to use instead of tuna, and it makes quite an elegant and tasty change.

The green peas are added for color as well as texture, and the cream of celery or mushroom soup—well, what can I say? Canned soups are incredibly high in sodium but they make the quickest, easiest sauce there is.

IF YOU'RE SO
INCLINED

If you'd rather not use canned soup, whether for reasons of health or for your reputation as a cook, make a homemade white sauce with a touch of celery seed.

And for an even fancier dish, you can pour the mixture into a casserole, top it with buttered bread crumbs, and bake it at 350° for half an hour.

Serves 4

1 pound wide egg noodles
One 10-ounce can cream of celery or mushroom soup
1 cup milk
One 10-ounce package frozen peas
One 15-ounce can pink salmon

1   Cook the egg noodles according to package directions in plenty of salted, boiling water.

2   When the noodles are done, drain and return them to the pan. Stir in the soup, milk, and peas. Bring to a boil. Reduce the heat and let the mixture simmer for 3 to 4 minutes until sauce has thickened a bit.

3   Drain the salmon and add it to the mixture. Stir gently to keep the salmon from turning to mush and to avoid breaking up the noodles. Heat thoroughly. Serve immediately.

Slow-Cooker Irish Stew

You might think of it as boring, but 240 million Americans of Irish descent can't be wrong! Irish stew is supposed to be thick, hearty, and flavorful; a melange of lamb chops and vegetables well-seasoned with salt, pepper, and a bit of thyme.

Unlike beef stew, which really needs the meat to be browned first, it's ideally suited to stewing in a slow cooker, which brings it to tender perfection. This dish does need to cook for a long time, but because it's in the slow cooker, it's completely unattended, so your hands-on time preparing it is under 10 minutes. Put it in the pot before you leave for work, and when you come home, it's as if a magic fairy got dinner ready.

Season with a generous hand. Irish stew should be pale but not bland.

Serves 4

2 medium onions

2 carrots

4 medium potatoes

2 pounds round-bone lamb chops

1 teaspoon salt

1 teaspoon dried thyme

1/2 teaspoon black pepper

2 beef stock cubes

Water

QUICK n PAINLESS

Cut your preparation time and make assembling this stew even faster by buying a bag of prescrubbed potatoes, that need nothing more than a quick rinse, and prepeeled carrots. Slice in the food processor with the onions and proceed.

1 Peel the onions, carrots, and potatoes and slice them into thick rounds on the slicing blade of the food processor.

2 Layer the lamb chops in the slow cooker with the vegetables. Sprinkle with salt, thyme, and pepper as you work.

3 Crumble the stock cubes on top and add water to cover, stirring the stock cubes in slightly. Put the lid on and cook on low for 8 to 10 hours (or on high for 4 to 5 hours).

IF YOU'RE SO
INCLINED

Lamb is the authentic meat for Irish stew, but you can also make a good version by substituting 2 pounds of stew beef, cut into 1-inch cubes (you can probably find pre-cut stew beef in the grocery store).

Chicken Pot Pie

This recipe relies almost entirely on commercial ingredients, not least of which is the meat from a rotisserie chicken (or left-over chicken meat from another dish), and yet the result is utterly delicious. You'll need a powdered biscuit mix (such as Bisquick) to make the topping. You can usually buy it in small amounts, packaged with just enough for 1 or 2 recipes, if you don't want a whole boxful.

The amount of butter is probably the secret to why this tastes so good, but the recipe works equally well with margarine. Cream of mushroom can replace the cream of celery, but the celery soup tastes delicious here, without adding an overt celery flavor.

You can put any canned vegetable in, but peas and/or carrots are the usual ones. You may be able to find them combined in one can, or you can use frozen—just add without thawing.

Serves 4 to 6

- 3 cups of cooked chicken (from 1 rotisserie or any pre-cooked chicken)
- 8 tablespoons (1 stick) butter or margarine
- 1 cup canned green peas and/or carrots
- 1 can cream of celery soup
- 1 cup water
- 1 cup biscuit mix
- 1 cup milk

IF YOU'RE SO INCLINED

If you don't have a rotisserie or other cooked chicken, the fastest way to get cooked chicken is to poach it. Put a whole raw chicken into a large saucepan. Cover it with cold water and bring to a boil over medium-high heat. Simmer for 30 to 40 minutes and remove to a plate. Allow to cool before removing the meat.

1 Preheat oven to 400°. Roughly chop the chicken meat into cubes. Melt the butter in a small cup in the microwave. If using canned vegetables, open the can and drain, holding the lid over the opening.

2 Put chicken across the bottom of a 9 × 13-inch glass casserole, and distribute the vegetables over the chicken.

3 In a medium bowl, whisk the condensed soup with the water, and pour over chicken and peas. Using the same bowl, whisk the biscuit mix with the milk and melted butter until smooth. Pour over the chicken.

4 Bake for 30 minutes, until crust is lightly browned and the casserole is bubbling around the edges. Cool for a few moments on top of the stove before serving.

Congratulations! You just made a chicken pot pie that's worthy of winning a county bake-off! Light a few candles and pour a couple glasses of cool white wine while your spouse nips up to the supermarket to buy a few pieces of chocolate torte. Forget about the canned soup in the recipe—you're dining in style tonight!

The Lazy Way

Speedy Shrimp Jambalaya

This traditional dish of New Orleans conjures up images of a sweaty cook hanging over a stew pot all day long, but with a few shortcuts, you can have a steaming, spicy pot of this soul-warming melange ready in less than 30 minutes.

Don't worry about the slightly longer list of ingredients—after you sauté the vegetables, everything else goes into the pot at once and bubbles away until the dish is ready. Using frozen shrimp is a big part of the speed, but when you're spooning up the deliciously fragrant sauce, you won't care a bit that you didn't just catch the shrimp in the bayou yourself.

Serves 4

2 medium onions

1 green bell pepper

2 ribs celery

2 tablespoons vegetable oil

2 cloves garlic

One 15-ounce can crushed tomatoes

1 1/2 cups water

1 chicken stock cube

1 teaspoon salt

1/2 teaspoon black pepper

1/2 teaspoon cayenne

1/2 teaspoon Old Bay seasoning (optional)

1 cup rice (uncooked)

1 pound large frozen shrimp, cleaned and deveined

IF YOU'RE SO INCLINED

Vary the jambalaya—or enrich the shrimp one—by adding other meats, such as ham cut into large cubes, diced cooked chicken, or any type of sausage. The authentic Louisiana recipe would include andouille sausage, but you could also add slices of kielbasa, or even spicy Italian sausage. If you want to use any raw meats instead of cooked ones, brown the meat with the vegetables before adding the other ingredients.

1 Chop the onions, pepper, and celery, using the food processor if you like. In large saucepan, heat the oil over medium heat and add the chopped vegetables, then pass the garlic through a garlic press directly into the pan.

2 Cook the vegetables for about 5 minutes, then add all the remaining ingredients. Stir well and bring to a boil.

3 Lower the heat, cover and simmer for about 25 minutes, until the rice is cooked through and most of the liquid has been absorbed. Taste and adjust seasonings.

QUICK ⟨ 'N' ⟩ PAINLESS

If you have leftover rice in the refrigerator, follow the recipe up to step 2, adding only ¹/₂ cup of water. Stir in the cooked rice in step 3 and let the jambalaya simmer for 7 to 10 minutes to heat through and thicken slightly.

Lazy Shepherd's Pie

Shepherd's Pie is something I rarely make until there's a cold wintry night when I want something warm and comforting. It may appear that the list of ingredients is long, but don't be put off—it can be thrown together in a big hurry and ends up being no extra effort.

The homey combination of hamburger and vegetables (including any leftovers in the fridge) under a thick blanket of mashed potatoes is warming and soothing. Grating the carrots is one of my lazy concessions, but I once resorted to using a can of mixed carrots, peas, and potatoes that mysteriously found its way into my pantry.

Instant mashed potatoes are my other big concession. I would never recommend that anyone use instant mashed potatoes for anything except Lazy Shepherd's Pie, where I doll them up with milk and extra butter, and also sprinkle them with cheese for a flavor boost. If you have leftovers of the real thing, use them instead, but if not, I think the time saved is worth the slight loss in flavor. Use a deep casserole dish. Shallow ones make you spread the potatoes too thin and the gravy leaks out.

Serves 4 to 6

1 pound hamburger

1 medium onion

2 medium carrots

6 cups instant mashed potatoes

2 tablespoons butter

1 tablespoon all-purpose flour

1 cup water

1 beef stock cube

1 cup frozen peas

1 tablespoon Worcestershire sauce

1 teaspoon salt

1/2 teaspoon black pepper

1/2 cup grated Cheddar cheese

1 Preheat the oven to 375°. In a large skillet, cook the hamburger over medium heat, breaking it up, until it starts to brown.

2 While the hamburger cooks, peel the onion and carrots and run them both through the grating blade of the food processor. Add vegetables to the meat and continue to cook until softened.

3 While the vegetables and meat are cooking, prepare the mashed potatoes according to package directions, using milk instead of water. Stir in the butter.

4 Sprinkle the flour over the meat and vegetables, and stir the mixture. Add the water and stock cube and bring to a boil.

5 Reduce the heat, and add green peas, Worcestershire sauce, salt, and pepper. Let it simmer for about 5 minutes until the sauce thickens slightly.

6 Pour the meat mixture into a deep 2-quart casserole dish and cover it with mashed potatoes. Sprinkle with cheese.

7 Bake for 25 to 30 minutes, until it is bubbling and browned.

YOU'LL THANK YOURSELF LATER

Casseroles such as Shepherd's Pie, which have potatoes as the main starch, freeze especially well. Compose two at once; freeze one, unbaked and without any toppings such as cheese or crumbs, to bake directly from the freezer.

Sausage and Spinach with Pasta

Here's another dish that could go into the oven to bake and bubble, but which I usually eat from the top of the stove as soon as it's hot and cooked through. Depending on the kind of sausage you use and whether you add chili flakes, you can make this dish spicy or mildly sweet, as you like.

Serves 4

1 pound round pasta, such as small shells or macaroni

1 pound Italian sausage, sweet or spicy

One 10-ounce package frozen spinach

2 tablespoons all-purpose flour

2 cups milk

1 teaspoon salt

$1/2$ teaspoon black pepper

$1/2$ teaspoon red chili flakes (optional)

Parmesan cheese

1   Cook the pasta according to directions in a large quantity of boiling, salted water.

2   While the pasta boils, cook the sausage in a skillet over medium heat. If it's in casings, simply squeeze it out into the pan and discard the casing. Cook the sausage thoroughly, breaking it up, until the edges start to brown, 7 to 8 minutes. (Note that with most Italian sausage, the meat may still appear pink due to the seasonings and preservatives in it.) Drain off and discard most of the fat.

3   While the sausage is cooking, put the spinach in a small bowl and microwave it on high until it's heated.

IF YOU'RE SO
INCLINED

Change the pasta shape and the vegetable and you have a whole new dish. Try this recipe with bow ties and broccoli, or spaghetti and sliced zucchini. If you don't have sausage, use hamburger and a teaspoon of dried whole oregano in its place, or leave out the meat altogether and enjoy the pasta and vegetables in a cream sauce.

4 Sprinkle the flour over the sausage and stir well. Cook for a minute or two, and then slowly stir in the milk, stirring well to prevent lumps from forming.

5 Add salt, pepper, and chili flakes and simmer gently, stirring frequently, until the sauce is thickened.

6 Add spinach and drained pasta to the skillet (or put the spinach and sausage in the pasta pan, if necessary) and toss well to combine. Heat through and serve immediately with generous toppings of Parmesan cheese.

QUICK n PAINLESS

If you happen to have fresh spinach in the house, it is just as easy to cook as frozen. Place the amount of spinach you need in a colander. Put the tea kettle on to boil, and when it whistles, pour the hot water over the spinach. It cooks in an instant!

Lazy Lasagna

It's hard to find someone who doesn't love lasagna. And it's equally hard to find a lazy way of making it. Ditch the prep work with no-cook lasagna noodles (a wonderful invention and available in most supermarkets in the pasta section), a pound of pregrated mozzarella, and a quart of the best quality commercial pasta sauce.

Using the no-cook lasagna noodles means that the dish has to bake a little longer, but with the astonishingly swift prep time, it's well worth it. You need all the sauce so that there's enough liquid to cook the noodles, so this lasagna may be a little juicier than you're used to. You may add a few more noodles than I call for here if you like more in your lasagna; I go sparingly on the noodles to speed things up.

Serves 6

2 cups cottage or ricotta cheese

2 large eggs

1/4 cup Parmesan (and extra for garnish, if desired)

One 32-ounce jar pasta sauce

1/2 of a 1-pound box no-cook lasagna noodles

One 16-ounce package grated mozzarella

1 Preheat the oven to 350°. In a small bowl, combine the cottage or ricotta cheese with the eggs and the Parmesan.

YOU'LL THANK YOURSELF LATER

It's hard to do anything to lasagna that makes it taste bad, but the quality of this one rides especially on the type of pasta sauce you buy. Try to get one without added sugar and starches. And you might want to buy a flavored one, such as the kind with mushrooms and peppers.

2 Make a layer of sauce (straight out of the jar, no need to heat it) in the bottom of a 2 quart casserole. Add 1 layer of noodles, then dollop on half of the cottage cheese mixture and top with a layer of mozzarella.

3 Repeat, ending with sauce. Add a sprinkle of Parmesan on top, if desired. Bake at 350° for 1 to 1½ hours. Test by sticking the point of a knife into the bubbling lasagna to see if the noodles are tender.

Congratulations! You just made a big tray of lasagna in less time than it would take a traditional Italian mama to get back from the market! Drink a big glass of red wine and light some candles while you eat—it's even better if you use a Chianti bottle as a candleholder.

The Lazy Way

Pita Pizza

There's no point in pretending that pizza isn't a one-dish meal. When you eat pizza, that's all you have. So it doesn't hurt to pile on a vegetable or two. And it's much cheaper and healthier to make your own at home now and then. But pizza lovers get disheartened by fake homemade versions. I've had the kind made with white bread, the kind made on packaged refrigerator biscuits, and the kind made on those big dry packaged crusts you can buy in the bakery sections of supermarkets. They're all a letdown.

Then I discovered pizza made on pita bread, and suddenly pizza for dinner became a possibility. The secret is in brushing the pita with olive oil to keep it from drying out. Hot pita has the chewy, bread-like taste of a proper pizza crust, and you can top it with anything from blanched vegetables to heaps of cheese and presliced pepperoni.

Makes 4 individual pizzas

1 bunch broccoli

$1/2$ cup black or green olives

Mozzarella (or try Monterey Jack, goat cheese, or Cheddar)

4 whole pita breads, white or whole wheat

Olive oil

One 8-ounce can tomato sauce

1 teaspoon dried oregano

Packaged presliced pepperoni (optional)

QUICK n PAINLESS

For an even speedier pizza, use frozen broccoli (cook them in the microwave first according to package directions), packaged grated cheese, and presliced pepperoni. You can also use a bottled pizza sauce, but tomato sauce with a sprinkle of oregano is cheaper and, surprisingly, gives a more authentic pizza-parlor flavor.

1 Preheat the oven to 350°. Trim the broccoli into small florets and discard the stem. Drop the broccoli into a saucepan of boiling water for 3 minutes, then drain.

2 Thinly slice the olives and grate the cheese.

3 Brush each pita with olive oil on front and back. Lay the pitas on a baking sheet and spread each one with 2 to 3 tablespoons of tomato sauce. Sprinkle 1/4 teaspoon of oregano on each.

4 Place the olives and pepperoni if using on the pitas and scatter the broccoli over the top. Put about 1/4 cup of cheese on the top of each.

5 Place the baking sheet in the oven and bake for 10 minutes until the cheese is melted and bubbly. Eat the pizza as soon as the cheese is cool enough to chew.

IF YOU'RE SO INCLINED

Since this pizza is made with pita bread, a Greek standard, why not make a Greek pizza? Use chopped tomato in place of the sauce, kalamata olives, and of course, a generous amount of feta cheese. Sprinkle on the oregano and drizzle with olive oil. Follow recipe directions for baking.

Getting Time on Your Side

	The Old Way	The Lazy Way
Making enough stew to feed a houseful of hungry teenagers	2 hours	30 minutes
Stewing up a rollicking pot of New Orleans jambalaya	2 hours	25 minutes
Building and baking a golden-crusted chicken pot pie	3 hours	40 minutes
Putting together a mashed potato-topped Shepherd's Pie	1 hour	15 minutes
Preparing and baking a big tray of cheesy lasagna	3 hours	1 1/2 hours
Making a one-pot meal you'd gladly invite guests to share	2 hours	30 minutes

Chapter thirteen

Meatless in Minutes: Pasta and Vegetarian Dishes on the Double

Meals without meat aren't just about being vegetarian, although, in some ways, vegetarians have it easier than carnivores—a well-stocked vegetarian pantry can keep the busy vegetarian going for up to two weeks without food-shopping. Root vegetables keep for a long time, and even broccoli and lettuce hold up well if they're kept dry and in the dark in the vegetable drawer. Pasta and rice will sit on the shelf for months—even years if necessary—as will canned beans and tomatoes. Most people usually have an egg or two and some cheese in the refrigerator for a quick omelet on a busy night.

You will find that a meatless kitchen is also less pressing about being attended to. Chicken breasts that you meant to cook last week will make their presence known before too many more days in the refrigerator, but celery and carrots will hold their peace for months and still remain serviceable (and sometimes even grow!).

Pasta will become one of your best friends, once you get used to quickly saucing it with out-of-the-ordinary toppings. Vegetables can be sliced, sautéed with onions, and tossed with pasta, Parmesan cheese, and a bit of the cooking water for a hearty and flavorful meal that's low-fat, too. If you have pesto in the refrigerator, you practically have dinner already made. Dried mushrooms only take a quick soak in hot water before they're ready for action, and canned beans can be heated with a little salsa and cumin in the 10 minutes it takes to cook a pot of rice. Grate a little cheese on top and you have the perfect protein, not to mention a satisfying meal.

The busy cook relies heavily on microwave baked potatoes as a side dish, but for a meatless meal, you'll also be well fed when baked potatoes are the main dish. Nuke the largest potatoes you can find, and slap them on the table with a carton of sour cream, a block of cheese, and a grater, for a real do-it-yourself meal. Chives and bacon bits are optional. For real lily-gilding, heat up a can of vegetarian chili or microwave some frozen chopped broccoli to spoon on top.

Today's vegetarians have pretty sophisticated palates, and there are a lot of creative ways to get meat off the dinner plate. Everyone's vegetarian now and then—with dishes like these, you may be vegetarian more often.

Hoppin' John

This is a traditional down-home Southern dish that is meant to be eaten on New Year's Day—along with collard greens—to ensure good luck for the rest of the year. It's made of black-eyed peas mixed with rice, and besides being delicious and filling, it has the added benefit of providing a great deal of protein.

It usually starts with dried black-eyed peas which cook down to a mushy consistency that blends well with the rice, but canned peas are faster and just as good, if a touch firmer. The red chili flakes are a traditional touch, and if you use the larger amount, your Hoppin' John will have a zesty bite.

Try serving with spinach, instead of collard greens, and a salad of fresh tomatoes and sliced onions, dressed with olive oil and vinegar.

Serves 3 to 4

One 16-ounce can black-eyed peas

1 1/2 cups raw rice

3 cups water

1 teaspoon salt

1/4 to 1/2 teaspoon red chili flakes

1. Drain the beans and put them in a large saucepan. Add the remaining ingredients and stir.

2. Bring to boil over high heat, then cover and reduce heat to medium-low. Cook for 20 minutes, without stirring, until the water has been absorbed and the rice is tender. Fluff with a fork and serve.

Congratulations! You've made a nutritious dinner full of protein and fiber in minutes. Since it's a Southern specialty, complete the meal with a slice of pecan pie—or maybe a frosty mint julep.

The Lazy Way

Puttanesca Pasta with Beans

"Puttana" is Italian for a woman practicing the world's oldest profession, and "puttanesca" is a style of quick-cooked pasta sauce—created by these ladies who need to be standing somewhere besides in front of the stove. The classic version has anchovies and olives, which replace slow-cooking with earthy flavors. This version adds a can of cannellini, the white kidney beans so favored by the Tuscans. Anchovies are optional here, but the flavor adds depth to the sauce.

It's a hearty, filling dish, halfway between the cooking of a puttana and some upright Italian mama, and the beans and pasta make a perfect protein. I'll bet those working girls would have had more energy to cook if they'd put beans in their sauce.

Serves 4 to 6

1 pound short tubular pasta shapes, such as rigatoni, penne, or even small shells

1/2 cup black olives (preferably from a deli or gourmet shop, not canned)

One 16-ounce can cannellini beans

2 tablespoons olive oil

4 to 5 cloves garlic

1 teaspoon red chili flakes

One 28-ounce can crushed tomatoes (try Italian plum)

4 whole anchovies, or 2 teaspoons anchovy paste (optional)

1 teaspoon dried oregano

Salt

A COMPLETE WASTE OF TIME

The 3 Worst Things to Do with Dried Beans:

1. Let them get too old on the shelf (like more than a year), so they'll never soften when cooked.

2. Add salt during cooking before they're tender.

3. Soak them. It's just not necessary, honestly. Put them in the slow cooker with some water and forget about them.

1. Cook the pasta in a large quantity of boiling salted water. Meanwhile, pit and roughly chop the olives; drain the beans.

2. In a large skillet, heat the olive oil over medium heat and push the garlic through a press directly into the oil. Add the chili flakes (don't breathe in over the hot pan as you do!), and stir for less than a minute until the garlic smells pungent.

3. Add the tomatoes and their juice, breaking them up with the back of a spoon. Stir in the anchovies or anchovy paste if using, the oregano, and the olives. Add the drained beans.

4. Bring it to a boil and bubble it hard for about 5 minutes until the sauce is slightly thickened. Taste and add salt.

5. Scoop some of the pasta cooking water into a cup and reserve. Drain the pasta. Add the pasta to the skillet (or pour the sauce into the pasta pan if your skillet isn't big enough). If it looks a little dry, stir in some of the pasta cooking water. Toss well and serve.

QUICK **n** PAINLESS

Many stores carry high-quality olives (not the flavorless canned ones!) that are already pitted. Make sure you're buying pitted olives if at all possible—if they only carry green pitted olives and not black pitted olives, buy the green! If your store does not carry good olives, use green cocktail olives, which taste better than canned black ones.

Spicy Peanut Noodles

Quick and savory, I eat this dish cold on hot nights, and hot on cold nights. It's filling and satisfying, and it can be ready as soon as the noodles are cooked, in about 10 minutes. Spicy Peanut Noodles keep well in the refrigerator and are excellent eaten right out of the container while you stand in the doorway of the fridge.

I only add the cucumber and bean sprouts: a) if I have them, and b) if I'm eating the dish right away. They don't hold up well for storing.

Serves 2 to 3

For noodles

1 pound Chinese egg noodles (or use vermicelli)

4 green onions

1 large cucumber (if eating dish right away)

2 cups fresh bean sprouts (if eating dish right away)

Cilantro (optional)

For sauce

1 cup peanut butter

1/2 cup hot water

1/4 cup cider vinegar

1/4 cup soy sauce

2 tablespoons sesame oil

1 clove garlic

1 teaspoon sugar

1 teaspoon red chili flakes

YOU'LL THANK YOURSELF LATER

Make a double batch of the spicy peanut sauce and store in the refrigerator. Use it for a new batch of noodles, with grilled chicken (which makes it into an Indonesian satay), or make a quick Asian slaw by pouring the sauce over cabbage shredded in the food processor. It also doubles as Indonesian Gado-Gado sauce to be poured over a hodgepodge salad of rice, hard-boiled eggs, bean sprouts, chopped green pepper, celery, carrots, etc.

1. Cook the noodles according to package directions. Meanwhile, chop the green onions—the white and green parts. If you want to add cucumber, peel and coarsely chop it.

2. While the noodles are cooking, place the sauce ingredients in a blender and puree them until smooth.

3. Drain the noodles and place them in a large serving bowl. Add the green onions, cucumber, and bean sprouts if using, and pour the sauce over all. Toss well, garnish with fresh cilantro, if desired, and eat it right away while it's warm, or store it covered in the refrigerator.

IF YOU'RE SO
INCLINED

Carnivores can make a very hearty meal out of this dish by adding 2 cups of diced cooked chicken to the noodles.

Creamy Mushroom Pasta

Fresh mushrooms take a bit of planning for busy cooks because we often find that the lovely white button mushrooms we bought on Saturday morning have turned into unappetizing brown chewy things with dark gills by Friday night. Dried mushrooms, however, are always ready and waiting for us to get around to them (my favorite dried mushrooms are shiitakes).

Fresh mushrooms have a delightful scent and mild flavor; dried ones have depth and earthiness, and a perfume that permeates an entire dish and lingers deliciously on the palate. In this lighter version of a creamy Pasta Alfredo, the woodsy flavor of shiitakes turns a rich side dish into a satisfying entree. Serve with a tartly dressed salad to lighten the meal.

Serves 4

2 ounces dried mushrooms, such as shiitake

1 pound long, thin pasta, such as fettucinne or spaghetti

1 small onion

2 cloves garlic

2 tablespoons olive oil

$1/2$ cup light cream

Salt and pepper

Parmesan cheese

1 Bring 2 cups of water to a boil in a bowl or Pyrex measuring cup in the microwave, about 3 minutes. Add mushrooms and let steep on the counter for 20 minutes.

2 At the same time, bring a large quantity of salted water for the pasta to boil on top of the stove. When the water boils, add the pasta.

YOU'LL THANK YOURSELF LATER

Make this dish lighter and lower in fat by following these instructions but leaving out the cream altogether. Simply toss the abbreviated sauce with the pasta, or blend in 1/4 cup of nonfat yogurt if desired, to thicken and smooth the sauce.

3 Dice the onion and mince the garlic. In a large skillet, heat the olive oil over medium heat. Add the onion and garlic and sauté for 2 to 3 minutes until they're slightly softened.

4 After the dried mushrooms have steeped, pour the mixture through a strainer lined with a paper towel, reserving the strained liquid into a small bowl or pyrex meauring cup. Pick off and discard the stems, which are woody, and chop the mushrooms.

5 Add the mushrooms and the strained soaking liquid to the skillet, and bring the mixture to a boil. Simmer for 5 minutes until the sauce is slightly reduced.

6 Pour in the cream and heat through. Season with salt and pepper.

7 Drain the pasta and place it in a large bowl. Pour the sauce over it, add a generous quantity of Parmesan, and toss well to combine. Serve immediately.

IF YOU'RE SO
INCLINED

If you have fresh mushrooms instead of dried, such as shiitake, cremini, or even plain white, thinly slice 1/2 pound of them, and sauté in the olive oil with the onion and garlic. Use chicken stock instead of the strained soaking liquid from dried mushrooms.

Pasta Salad

Cold salads made of pasta exploded on the American culinary scene in the 80's and never left. From a time when every restaurant offered its version as a side dish to a time when a restaurant that serves it seems hopelessly retro, pasta salad is still a favorite for picnics, light lunches and suppers, and potluck meals. Like chili, every cook has a recipe for pasta salad.

My favorite version is a classic lazy compromise that uses a small selection of fresh vegetables, quickly blanched in the same water in which the pasta cooks, but dressed with a good-quality bottled Italian dressing (although it certainly tastes best with a fresh, homemade vinaigrette, if you have the energy). I like to use broccoli and carrots, which don't become mushy (asparagus is also terrific if it's in season). These vegetables also keep well in the refrigerator, unlike fresh tomatoes and cucumbers, which become watery and limp if you store the salad for a few days—or even overnight. It makes a good brown bag lunch if you have a refrigerator at work.

Serves 4 to 6

- 1 pound tricolored rotini (or any short, round shapes such as macaroni or penne)
- 1 medium bunch broccoli
- 1 large carrot
- 1 bottle good-quality Italian salad dressing
- 1/4 cup green olives (optional)
- 1/4 cup Parmesan cheese (optional)

QUICK n' PAINLESS

Pasta salad from supermarket salad bars can be soggy and overdressed—better to make your own. But you can buy prechopped fresh vegetables from a salad bar. Take one container for harder vegetables such as cauliflower, broccoli, and squash, so you can quickly blanch them in the pasta water; take another one for snow peas, mushrooms, and baby corn, which can be added to the salad directly (be sure to use them that night).

1. Cook the pasta in a large quantity of salted boiling water according to package directions. Don't overcook—if there was ever a time for al dente pasta, it's now.

2. While the pasta is cooking, trim the broccoli into bite-size florets. (Ideally, you should peel and slice the stem, but hey, it's easier to throw it away.) Peel the carrot and slice it into thin disks, about 1/8" thick.

3. Just before the end of the pasta's cooking time, add the carrots and broccoli to the cooking water and return it to a boil. Let it cook less than 2 minutes until the vegetables soften just slightly and the pasta is al dente. Dump it into a colander and run cold water over all. Drain well.

4. Place the pasta and vegetables in a large bowl and add dressing. Start with about half the bottle and add more if desired. Toss lightly to coat. If using olives, slice them and add to the pasta with the Parmesan cheese. You can eat it now or chill for a couple of hours. Store it tightly covered in a glass or plastic container in the refrigerator.

IF YOU'RE SO
INCLINED

Make a classic home-made dressing by mixing 1/2 cup extra-virgin olive oil with 1/4 cup red wine vinegar. Shake it up in a jar with 1/2 teaspoon of oregano, 1 clove of garlic, minced, and a dash of salt and pepper.

Fritatta

I'd like you to meet fritatta, unless the two of you are already intimate. More solidly filling than an omelet, a frittata has the virtue of being less ephemeral as well. True, omelets are the ideal lazy dinner, but it's hardly practical to make them for more than two people unless you like to feed your family assembly-line style. Frittatas are more like a thick egg cake. They can be served hot, at room temperature, or even cold from the fridge. They can be filled with absolutely anything: from chopped cooked greens, to diced leftover potatoes, to grated cheese, to minced-up, leftover pork roast. Following is a green frittata recipe to get you started, but let your conscience and your vegetable drawer be your guide.

There is one problem with frittatas: Although few cooks have the expertise to flip them whole, it's necessary to cook the top as well as the bottom. Many cooks settle for finishing the frittata under the broiler, but I never remember to heat the broiler. I find the laziest option is to slip the partially cooked frittata onto a plate and flip it upside down back into the pan.

Serves 4

1 small onion

1 red pepper

One 10-ounce box frozen chopped spinach

2 tablespoons olive oil

6 large eggs

1/4 cup Parmesan (optional)

1 teaspoon salt

1/2 teaspoon black pepper

IF YOU'RE SO INCLINED

Frittatas can be made with lots of ingredients, as in this recipe, or with a very few. Try making frittata with nothing but a handful of chopped fresh basil leaves, some mushrooms sautéed in butter, or with a small jar of artichoke hearts, drained.

1 Dice the onion and red pepper. Put the spinach package in a bowl and zap it on high in the microwave for 3 to 4 minutes.

2 Meanwhile, heat the olive oil over medium heat in a medium skillet, preferably nonstick. Sauté the onion and pepper for 2 to 3 minutes.

3 Drain off any liquid from the spinach package, open it, and add the thawed spinach to the skillet. Cover the skillet, increase the heat slightly, and cook until the spinach is tender, about 5 minutes.

4 While the vegetables are cooking, beat the eggs with the Parmesan if using, salt, and pepper in the same bowl in which you nuked the spinach. Mixing as you pour, add the eggs to the skillet. When the ingredients are well combined, let the mixture cook without stirring for several minutes until the bottom is firmly set. Do not break up the eggs.

5 When the frittata is mostly firm, slip it out, bottom-side down, onto a serving plate. Flip it back into the pan, top-side down, and cook another 1 to 2 minutes until the frittata is firm on both sides but not especially brown. Put it back on the plate and serve as desired.

QUICK ⬛ PAINLESS

To skip the flipping technique, preheat the broiler in time. Once the ingredients are well combined (step 4), turn on the broiler to heat up as you cook the bottom of the fritatta. Then just place the pan under the heat to brown the top. (Just make sure the handle of your pan is oven proof!)

IF YOU'RE SO
INCLINED

To make it a really filling meal or to stretch it for a crowd, put 1/2 a cup of cooked white rice into the bottom of each bowl before spooning in the lentil stew. Garnish with diced tomatoes, a sprinkle of chopped peanuts, or some chopped fresh parsley—or all three.

Lentil Stew

Make this on the stovetop if you're going to be around, or let it simmer in a slow cooker all day if you're not. It's astonishingly easy, and the result is an elaborately delicious and filling stew, packed with protein and nutrients and a lot of fiber to boot.

Serve it with sourdough bread to pick up the hint of tanginess from the lemon juice that you squeeze in just before serving.

Serves 4 to 6

2 onions

2 ribs celery

2 large carrots

4 to 5 cloves garlic

3 cups brown lentils

One 16-ounce can chopped tomatoes

1 teaspoon dried oregano

1 bay leaf

2 teaspoons salt

1 teaspoon black pepper

1 lemon

1 Peel as necessary and coarsely chop the onions, celery, carrots, and garlic.

2. Combine all ingredients except the lemon in a large stew pot and cover with 2 quarts of cold water. Bring to a boil, reduce heat, cover loosely, and simmer gently over a very low heat for 3 to 4 hours. (If you use a slow cooker, place all of the ingredients except the lemon in the cooker, add 2 quarts of water, and leave on high for 8 to 10 hours.)

3. When the stew is thick, and the lentils and vegetables are tender (the vegetables will cook down to a sort of mush), half the lemon and squeeze the juice into the stew (use a strainer or squeeze the juice through your fingers to catch the seeds). Stir and adjust the seasoning with salt and pepper. Add more lemon juice if desired.

YOU'LL THANK YOURSELF LATER

This stew stores very well in the refrigerator and freezer. If you have leftovers, or perhaps made this recipe before you received an invitation to the hot new restaurant you've been dying to go to, scoop it into plastic containers and pop in the freezer. Simply thaw and heat in the microwave for a quick supper.

IF YOU'RE SO
INCLINED

To make a simple eggplant Parmigiana, top each eggplant steak with just a dollop of tomato sauce and a slice of mozzarella cheese. Put back under the heat for just a minute to melt, but not brown, the cheese, and serve right away. Save leftovers to heat in the microwave and make into a sandwich on a sliced baguette.

Eggplant Steaks in Tomato Sauce

Cut thick and broiled, these slices of eggplant have a crisp outside and delectably creamy inside. Don't cut them too thin, or the interiors won't be thick enough to get creamy. Presented on a simple bed of tomato sauce with a hint of oregano, they provide a winning centerpiece on a dinner plate.

Serves 4

2 small to medium eggplants

1/4 cup olive oil

2 cloves garlic

Salt and pepper

One 16-ounce can tomato sauce

1/4 teaspoon whole dried oregano

1 Preheat the broiler and line the broiler pan with foil to ease cleaning. Trim the top and bottom off the eggplants, and slice them into 1/2- to 3/4-inch thick slices. Place on broiler pan.

2 Put the olive oil into a cup or small bowl and pass the garlic through a press directly into the cup. Use a pastry brush to stir the garlic and oil, then paint this oil onto each side of the eggplant slices.

3 Sprinkle the slices with salt and pepper and broil for 3 to 5 minutes on each side, until well browned but not burned.

4 While the eggplant is broiling, put the tomato sauce in a small saucepan, stir in the oregano, and warm over medium heat until heated through.

5 To serve, spoon a puddle of tomato sauce onto each plate and lay slices of broiled eggplant on top.

Speedy Burritos

If you've got flour tortillas, bottled salsa, and a can of beans, you're halfway to dinner. Burritos are amazingly forgiving. You can make them out of practically anything, from scrambled eggs, to chili, to fried potato and onion. This recipe is for a more traditional version.

Serves 2

1 tablespoon olive oil

One 16-ounce can black beans or pinto beans

1 teaspoon cumin

1 ripe avocado

Cheese

Lettuce

Four 8-inch flour tortillas

Salsa

1. In a large skillet, heat the olive oil over medium-low heat. Drain the beans, dump into the skillet, and stir, mashing half the beans with the back of a spoon. Stir in the cumin and continue to heat gently.

2. Peel and dice the avocado. Grate some cheese. Thinly slice some lettuce.

3. Wrap the flour tortillas in a clean kitchen towel or in plastic wrap. Lay the wrapped tortillas on a plate and heat them in the microwave on high for 45 seconds.

4. Spoon a quarter of the beans down the middle of a heated tortilla. Sprinkle cheese over the hot beans, add some shredded lettuce and diced avocado, and spoon on salsa to taste. Roll up the burritos and eat them right away.

QUICK n' PAINLESS

Slice the avocado all the way around the long way and twist to pull apart. One side will have the large pit. Holding it in one hand, tap the pit with the sharp edge of your knife blade. The blade will stick into the pit enough to let you twist it out with ease. If the skin doesn't peel off easily, scoop the avocado out with a spoon and chop the scooped flesh.

Getting Time on Your Side

	The Old Way	The Lazy Way
Creating a fragrant bean and pasta stew with complex depths and undertones of flavor	3 hours	20 minutes
Time to cook Southern classic bean and rice dish, Hoppin' John	3 hours	20 minutes
Concocting Eggplant Parmigiana	1 hour	15 minutes
Carefully trimming all the vegetables for pasta salad	15 minutes	0 minutes
Assembling and preparing ingredients to make burritos	1 hour	10 minutes
Time that an elaborately constructed dish of delicate eggs and vegetables can sit before it's ruined	1 minute (omelet)	24 hours (frittata!)

Chapter

fourteen

It's Easy Being Green: Veggies, Salads, and Sides

Plain green salad is the busy cook's standard vegetable. It's a serviceable fallback and always at the ready because it requires little more than the rinsing and tearing of a few lettuce leaves. It's easy to add a few ingredients such as carrots, cucumbers, or fresh tomatoes if you need a bit of color; and making a tasty vinaigrette takes about 30 seconds more than dragging a bottled dressing from the fridge.

Although a green salad is the simplest all-purpose accompaniment to many a dish, its appearance night after night may make you and your fellow diners yearn for more, especially in the summer, when there is a preponderance of fresh vegetables.

So smart cooks take advantage of what's in season to save work. When corn was ripe and tomatoes were bursting with freshness, my mother (who has flashes of lazy inspiration) would occasionally serve us nothing but boiled corn and sliced tomatoes for supper, with nothing on the side but butter and salt. It always felt like a celebration.

Don't get trapped in the frozen vegetable cycle. Although they have their place (I find frozen peas, corn, and spinach especially useful), fresh vegetables are usually faster to cook and much, much tastier, especially if you can find organic vegetables in your local market. Any type of squash (such as zucchini or yellow crookneck) can be thinly sliced and sautéed quickly in olive oil with a mashed clove of garlic. And since green beans should have the slight crunch that comes from a 5-minute dip in boiling water (the same is true for broccoli), cooking these nutritious green couldn't be faster or easier.

If the idea of steamed, boiled, or even sautéed vegetables sounds boring, a dash of soy sauce here and there, a nip of garlic, the judicious use of butter and lemon juice can work wonders. Vegetables are easy to leave off the plate, so be careful not to fall into the habit of sizzling a steak and eating it with nothing but buttered noodles. According to current government nutrition charts, we should all eat at least 5 servings of fruits and vegetables every day, for the fiber as much as for the vitamins.

And vegetables are not just for your health, either—they add color and texture to a meal, and they're delicious, especially when prepared with a little care. Why lavish all the attention on the meat alone? You'll be well repaid for the few extra moments you take to make your vegetables an equal part of the meal with your meat and starch. The vegetables and salads that follow have the same approximate cooking times of most main dishes in this book, so that you can start cooking the meat, then work on the vegetable while the meat cooks (or vice versa), and they'll be ready at about the same time.

Fresh vegetables are always my preference whenever possible. Steam, sauté, boil, or grill your plain fresh vegetables—we'll go over the basic techniques that you can use for any vegetable. When cooking frozen ones, you may want to add garlic or sesame seeds to perk up the flavor. Combine several you have on hand, and do whatever you need to vegetables and toss lightly with butter and fresh parsley to make them look and taste festive.

Once you get into composed salads and vegetable dishes, such as Lazy Potato Salad and Asian Slaw, let your imagination take over. Add whatever you have on hand, and do whatever you need to do to get your full complement of veggies. We busy cooks are not bound by the same culinary laws as others—if our children want ketchup on broccoli because "it might taste nice," we say, "Great! Whatever gets you to eat it!"

COOKING VEGGIES

Sautéed Vegetables

Tender vegetables, especially green ones, benefit most from being sautéed. I sauté zucchini, spinach, snow peas, summer squash, peppers, and mushrooms. You can use olive oil or butter or a combination of the two, but avoid regular cooking oil, which doesn't add any flavor to the food. I've used zucchini in the recipe below, but you can substitute any tender, succulent vegetable for the zucchini.

Sautéed Zucchini

Serves 4

4 to 5 small to medium zucchini
2 to 3 tablespoons olive oil or butter
1 clove garlic (optional)
Salt and freshly ground black pepper

1. Rinse and slice the zucchini into very thin slices or matchsticks.

2. Heat the olive oil or butter (or a combination of the two) in a large skillet over medium heat. Press the garlic, if using, through a garlic press directly into the pan. Add the sliced zucchini immediately.

3. Stir until the zucchini is coated with the oil and leave to cook for 5 to 10 minutes, stirring occasionally. When the zucchini turns limp and tender, with a few browning edges, sprinkle with salt and pepper and serve.

A COMPLETE WASTE OF TIME

The 3 Worst Things to Do with Fresh Vegetables:

1. Store them in overly moist conditions (like in a wet bag) so mold can grow.

2. Overcook them so they're mushy, pale, and flavorless (or too potent, like sulfurous overcooked cabbage).

3. Forget about them, not eat them, and throw them away every couple of weeks, to be replaced by a new crop.

Braised Vegetables

Braising is for vegetables that need an extra bit of moist cooking that sautéing can't provide. Leeks, radicchio, asparagus, celery, Belgian endive, fennel, carrots, and others can be braised with excellent results and not a lot of prep work. You can simply split and clean leeks and endive, lightly chop Swiss chard and radicchio, leave asparagus whole, halve stalks of celery, and cut fennel into slices. I like butter for braising, because as the liquid cooks away, it forms a sort of glaze on the vegetables.

Braised Leeks

Serves 4

1 pound leeks

2 tablespoons butter or olive oil

$1/2$ to $3/4$ cup water

$1/2$ teaspoon salt

Freshly ground black pepper

1 Cut the roots and all of the tough green tops off the leeks, leaving only the white and the most tender green part. Slice them in half lengthwise and rinse, making sure to get any grit out.

2 In a large saucepan, heat the butter or olive oil over medium heat. Add the leeks and stir to coat. Cook for about 5 minutes, then pour in the water and add salt and pepper.

3 Cover loosely and simmer very gently for 15 to 20 minutes, until the leeks are tender and most of the water has evaporated.

IF YOU'RE SO
INCLINED

You can braise vegetables in other liquids besides water. Try an equal amount of chicken stock—or water and a stock cube—as well as beef stock, white wine, and even red wine for strong flavored veggies such as leeks.

Grilled Vegetables

If you have a gas grill right outside the back door or on a balcony, you can grill vegetables anytime with ease, either as a side dish or for a whole meal. Grilled veggies are great plain, with a vinaigrette, or on a sandwich, either as the star ingredient or a topping. Grilling is good for a wide range of vegetables, from asparagus to zucchini, including peppers, eggplant, onion, and summer squash. You can even grill slices of potato if you have the patience to wait for them to soften (I usually don't). Whatever you grill, be sure to give it a thin brushing of oil first, and to slice thick veggies (like eggplant and onion) to an even thinness. This recipe calls for eggplant, zucchini, and onion.

Grilled Eggplant, Zucchini, and Onion

Serves 4

1 medium eggplant

1 medium zucchini

2 large onions

Olive oil

Salt and freshly ground black pepper

Balsamic vinegar (optional)

1. Preheat grill to medium high. Slice the eggplant and zucchini lengthwise into slice 1/2-inch thick slices. Peel the onion and cut into rings 3/4-inch thick.

QUICK ⬤ PAINLESS

When you're just not quite sure what to do with those grilled veggies or perhaps have leftovers, for a fast and flavorful meal pile them on top of store-bought focaccia, which can be found nowadays at most deli counters in supermarkets. Since the focaccia already has sauce and seasonings on it, when topped with grilled veggies it's a gourmet pizza fit for a king.

2 Use a pastry brush to coat vegetables on both sides with olive oil. Sprinkle with salt and pepper and lay on the hot grill, closer to the edges (avoid placing over direct heat).

3 Grill for about 5 minutes on each side, perhaps longer according to the heat of your grill, until the vegetables are softened and dark brown but not black. Remove to a serving platter and drizzle with more olive oil and some balsamic vinegar, if desired. Serve hot or cold.

IF YOU'RE SO INCLINED

Grilling is much faster than roasting for browning vegetables and bringing out their natural sweetness. But if you're already roasting a whole chicken or a piece of meat, you may want to add a separate pan of vegetables (putting them in the same pan slows cooking and soaks your veggies in grease). Cut potatoes, carrots, and onions into large chunks and toss with a tablespoon or two of olive oil in a shallow glass casserole. Sprinkle with salt and pepper and roast on a high rack for 45 minutes to 1 hour, until browned and tender (the oven should be from 350° to 400°). When you baste the roasting meat, you may want to add a few spoonfuls of its juices to the vegetable pan.

Steamed Vegetables

Steaming leaves colors brighter and flavors stronger and fresher, and it's ideal for broccoli and cauliflower, as well as carrots, Brussels sprouts, and asparagus (which you may want to cut into thirds to fit in a steamer basket). Although a metal steamer basket that fits down in the saucepan makes the job easy, you can also do a modified version of steaming by setting the raw vegetables into about ¾-inch of water and covering tightly. The parts on the bottom, in contact with the water, will boil, but the rest will steam. Here's a recipe for steamed cauliflower—again, feel free to try other veggies.

Steamed Cauliflower

Serves 4

1 large head cauliflower
1/2 cup water
Salt and freshly ground pepper

1 Break the cauliflower into florets or leave it whole.

2 Place the water in the bottom of a large saucepan. (You may need more to make it about 1/2-inch deep, but don't overfill.)

3 Bring water to a boil and add the cauliflower, either in the steamer basket or directly to the pan. Cover tightly and steam for 7 to 10 minutes, until cauliflower is tender. If the water starts to boil away, add a bit more.

4 Remove cauliflower from basket or pan. Season with salt and pepper and serve.

COMPOSED SALADS AND VEGETABLE DISHES

Summer Tomato Salad

The fastest salad possible is sliced summer tomatoes topped with a few torn leaves of fresh basil. It's sheer indulgence to put slices of fresh mozzarella between the slices of tomato, but it's delicious, and makes for a beautiful, impressive platter that only took you moments to make.

Only make this when you have the freshest, ripest summer tomatoes, not the pale, hard tomatoes of winter. Use any kind you have, but my favorite is big slices of juicy beefsteak tomato. If you can, buy fresh mozzarella, the soft white kind, not the firm yellow kind that comes packaged in plastic. Otherwise, leave it out. The salad is still good.

Serves 4

3 to 4 large ripe tomatoes

8 ounces fresh mozzarella

Handful of fresh basil leaves

1/4 cup extra-virgin olive oil

3 tablespoons balsamic vinegar (or red wine vinegar)

Salt and freshly ground black pepper

1 Core the tomatoes and slice them thickly. Place on a large serving platter. Slice the mozzarella and distribute the pieces among the tomato slices.

2 Tear the basil leaves off their stems and scatter them over the tomatoes. Drizzle the platter with olive oil and vinegar and sprinkle with salt and pepper. Serve at room temperature.

Congratulations! You just made a classic and tempting Italian summer salad in minutes. Go for a stroll in the park after dinner and treat yourself to a fruity gelato to continue the Italian theme of your evening!

The Lazy Way

Winter Cucumber Salad

In winter, cucumbers are always available to make a fast fresh salad. Scrub the cucumbers well, but you don't have to peel them unless the skin is very shiny. If so, they're probably heavily waxed and should be peeled.

Serves 4

2 medium cucumbers

1 small yellow onion

2 tablespoons red wine vinegar

2 tablespoons sour cream or plain yogurt

1/2 teaspoon salt

Freshly ground black pepper

1 Scrub or peel the cucumbers, peel the onion, and slice them thinly, or (more quickly) run them through a thin-slicing blade on a food processor. Place sliced onion and cucumber in a medium bowl.

2 Add remaining ingredients. Toss and serve.

Asian Slaw

As far as I'm concerned, the food processor was made for slaw. You can reduce a head of cabbage to a quivering heap of shreds in about 30 seconds (to achieve the same fineness with a knife, it may take you an hour or something). If you want carrots, switch to the grating blade and whizzz: grated carrot. This Asian-inspired, sesame-accented dressing makes a nice change from American slaw. It also stores well.

Serves 4 to 6

$^1/_2$ head cabbage (white, green, red, Savoy, anything)

2 carrots (optional)

$^1/_2$ cup rice wine vinegar (or cider vinegar)

3 tablespoons sesame oil

3 tablespoons soy sauce

1 tablespoon sugar

1 heaping tablespoon ground ginger

3 tablespoons sesame seeds (optional)

$^1/_2$ cup salted peanuts (optional)

$^1/_2$ cup fresh cilantro (optional)

1 Shred the cabbage and grate the carrots if using in the food processor. Place them in a large mixing bowl.

2 In a small cup, mix the vinegar, sesame oil, soy sauce, sugar, and ginger, or shake them in a tightly lidded jar. Pour over the cabbage and toss well to coat.

3 If you use sesame seeds, toast them first by shaking them in a dry skillet over high heat for 30 seconds. Then sprinkle them on top. Garnish with chopped salted peanuts and cilantro, if desired.

QUICK ᴨ PAINLESS

Skip the elaborate Asian-influenced dressing on a busy night. Shred the cabbage and carrots in a food processor and mix with some mayonnaise and lemon juice. Slaw in minutes—break out the hot dogs!

You can use this lazy method to make American potato salad as well, if you don't mind unpeeled potatoes (which really taste better). Put small new potatoes in a saucepan of cold water along with a couple of eggs. Bring to a boil. Remove the eggs after 10 minutes. Continue cooking the potatoes until they're tender. Rinse the eggs and potatoes with cold water, and chill. When they're cold, cut the spuds in half, peel and dice the eggs, and dress all with mayonnaise spiked with vinegar and yellow mustard. Add onion, celery, pickles, etc., as desired.

Lazy Potato Salad

When you make potato salad, whether it's French or Italian vinaigrette style or American-style with mayonnaise, the potatoes have to be cooked with the skin on to keep them from getting mushy. I usually make the former, because the American style is so labor-intensive, what with boiling, cooling, peeling, slicing, etc.

Gourmets believe in getting the dressing—or at least the vinegar—onto the potatoes while they're still as hot as can be, which means peeling the steaming hot spuds by hand while they're still scalding. There was a day when I would attempt such a thing, rubber gloves and all, but gradually I came to realize that life just might be too short for such things. Now, not only do I not cut them into tempting little bite-size pieces, I don't even peel the potatoes at all, and I'm sure I'm the better for it. (All the vitamins are in the skin, you know.)

This whole-spud approach can only be done, of course, if you have tiny potatoes, so buy the littlest new potatoes you can find. The red-skinned ones look nice in the following salad. You may want to double this recipe because it's great to have leftovers. The dressing here is the standard vinaigrette that I throw together for any green salad, with or without garlic, but don't skimp on the Dijon, which holds the whole thing together and makes the texture creamy.

Serves 4

1$1/2$ pounds new potatoes
$1/2$ pound fresh green beans

Dressing

1 clove garlic

1/2 cup olive oil

1/4 cup red wine vinegar

3 tablespoons Dijon mustard

1/2 teaspoon salt

1/2 teaspoon black pepper

1. Scrub any dirt off the potatoes and put them in a large saucepan. Cover with cold water and add a couple of teaspoons of salt. Bring to a boil over medium heat and cook until tender and the skins just start to crack, 10 to 15 minutes.

2. While the potatoes are cooking, snap the ends off the green beans and break them into bite-size lengths. Before the end of the potato-cooking time, add the green beans and cook them until they're bright green but still crunchy, 3 to 5 minutes.

3. While the beans and potatoes finish cooking, make the dressing. Push the garlic through a press into a small jar with a tightly fitted lid. Add the remaining dressing ingredients and shake hard until the dressing is thick and creamy.

4. Drain the beans and potatoes, and place them in a large serving bowl. Pour dressing over all and toss well to coat. Eat right away or let cool for several hours. Store, covered, in the refrigerator.

YOU'LL THANK YOURSELF LATER

Make a double batch of the dressing and store half in the refrigerator to use on a green salad, or as a marinade for chicken breasts. (Be sure to discard any marinade after soaking meat in it!)

Greek Salad

If you have black olives in the pantry and feta cheese in the fridge, you've got the fixings for Greek Salad. There are garnishes such as anchovies and stuffed grape leaves out of a jar, but most of us are looking for the cheese and olives, along with the oregano-scented dressing. Lettuce, red onions, and cucumbers make up the vegetable part, but I've seen perfectly acceptable Greek Salads that have only two out of the three. If you don't have lettuce, the red onion and cucumber version makes a more relish-like salad. Green peppers are less traditional but also very tasty, if you have them on hand.

Serves 2

1/2 small head romaine lettuce

1 medium cucumber

1 small red onion

1/2 cup feta cheese

1/2 cup black olives (preferably Kalamata)

For dressing

1/2 cup olive oil

1/4 cup red wine vinegar or lemon juice

1 teaspoon dried oregano

1/2 teaspoon salt

1/2 teaspoon black pepper

Once a week, wash and dry lots of lettuce in your salad spinner. Minimalist salads need a little color and crunch, so lose the iceberg habit—use romaine, Bibb, curly red, and frisee. Tear the lettuce into bite-size pieces. (Don't cut it! The leaves will wilt more quickly.) Line a big plastic bag (I use a clean grocery store bag) with paper towels and fill it with premixed salad. Your salad will stay crisp and be ready to eat in a hurry.

1. Rinse and tear the lettuce leaves. Peel and thinly slice the cucumber (or cut it into cubes). Peel and thinly slice the red onion.

2. Place the lettuce in a salad bowl, and arrange the cucumber and onion on top. Sprinkle with cheese and olives.

3. Place the dressing ingredients in a jar with a tight fitting lid and shake hard. Pour evenly over the salad and serve.

QUICK ☜ PAINLESS

For a lightning speed lunch, stuff this salad into a pita pocket. If you're bringing this to work, pack the dressing separately, even in a zipperlock bag, and pour on right before eating, so the veggies don't get soggy.

Simple Celeri Remoulade

The classic French salad made from celery root, or celeriac, involves julienning a big ugly celery root extremely thinly. These matchsticks are covered in a dressing that is heavy on the Dijon mustard, and then left overnight or at least several hours until the celery root wilts somewhat. It's a wonderful salad; the mildly nutty white celery root is sharply flavored by the dressing, but it's far too much work for the busy cook. I resolved never to julienne another piece of celeriac; when one would come into my possession I'd cook it in chunks with potatoes and mash them together (which is also very nice).

But at the back of my mind, I wondered why we busy people should be denied Celeri Remoulade. And as I pondered this one day, my eye fell on the food processor. And not long after that, I was happily dressing a large mound of freshly grated celery root. Grating the celeriac means that you don't have to let the salad marinate to soften. It might make classic French chefs groan in agony, so just don't invite them to dinner.

Serves 4 to 6

1 large celery root

For dressing

1 lemon

1/2 cup olive oil

3 tablespoons Dijon mustard

1/2 teaspoon salt

1/2 teaspoon black pepper

A COMPLETE WASTE OF TIME

The 3 Worst Things to Do with Green Salad:

1. Dress it any sooner than immediately before serving.

2. Serve it on the same warm plates as the entree.

3. Put dressing on more lettuce than you need and then try to store the dressed leaves.

1   Cut the celery root in half and store half for another use (it's terrific in mashed potatoes). Use a paring knife to cut the thick peel off the celeriac, including any knobby roots. Working quickly to keep the flesh from browning, cut it into chunks that you can feed into the food processor with the grating blade in place. Place the grated celeriac in a mixing bowl.

2   Juice the lemon directly into a jar with a tight fitting lid (catching the seeds) and add the remaining dressing ingredients. Shake until creamy and pour it over the grated celery root. Toss well to combine. Taste, and add more salt or lemon juice, if needed.

YOU'LL THANK YOURSELF LATER

This is one of the few raw veggie salads that actually benefits from sitting overnight. Make it one day and plan to eat it the next. Stored tightly covered in the refrigerator overnight, the crisp celeriac softens in the tangy dressing and the flavor becomes creamier. Stir it up before serving.

Sesame Broccoli

As a child, I found broccoli among the least offensive of vegetables, so my mother fed it to me frequently, and consequently, though I didn't hate it, I got sick and tired of it.

It was a happy day when I met Sesame Broccoli in a Chinese restaurant. Soy sauce and toasted sesame oil don't mask the flavor; they heighten it. And so far, I haven't tired of Sesame Broccoli.

Serves 2

1 large bunch broccoli
1 clove garlic
2 tablespoons soy sauce
1 tablespoon sesame oil
2 teaspoons sesame seeds

1 Bring a pot of salted water to a boil. Trim the broccoli into long florets, including the stems. When the water is boiling, drop in the broccoli and cook for about 5 minutes until it's tender but still bright green (not the dark green of overcooked broccoli).

2 Push the garlic through a press into a serving bowl. Add the soy sauce, sesame oil, and sesame seeds. Stir the dressing with a fork.

3 When the broccoli is cooked, drain it well and add it to the serving bowl. Toss to coat with dressing. This is as good at room temperature as it is piping hot.

Rapid Ratatouille

Ratatouille doesn't have to be the all-day affair of a Provençal housewife. Ratatouille for two is more than twice as fast as ratatouille for four, so if you're going to double the recipe, don't expect it to be rapid.

Serves 2

- 1 medium eggplant
- 1 medium zucchini
- 1 red bell pepper
- 3 tablespoons olive oil
- 2 cloves garlic
- 1 large fresh tomato (or 1 cup canned whole tomatoes, with juice)
- Salt and pepper
- Fresh basil (optional)

1. Coarsely dice the eggplant. Slice the zucchini into thin rings. Core and seed the pepper and cut into thin strips.

2. In a large skillet, heat the olive oil over medium heat. Push the garlic through a press into the hot oil and add the chopped vegetables. Sauté for 5 minutes.

3. For fresh tomato, coarsely chop on a cutting board and scrape the flesh and juices into the pan. If you use canned tomatoes, break them up with a spoon as you add them.

4. Bring the mixture to a boil, reduce heat, and simmer gently for 5 to 7 minutes until the vegetables are tender, and the tomato is cooked down and slightly thickened.

5. Season well with salt and pepper. Add coarsely chopped basil leaves just before serving.

QUICK ⬤ PAINLESS

Make a point of buying quick-cooking vegetables such as fresh spinach, snow peas, peas, zucchini, green onions, and summer squash. Succulent vegetables tend to cook faster, and tender greens don't need to stew like turnip greens. Spinach cooks in minutes if you rinse it and toss it in a hot pan with nothing more than the water clinging to the leaves.

Mashed Carrots and Parsnips

Warming, filling, and colorful, this is a sweet mash of root vegetables that many people are surprised to find that they like even when they don't like carrots and parsnips. Together, they have a rich, buttery flavor—without any butter being added. The cooked carrots and parsnips won't mash together into a completely smooth, pale orange puree, but will retain their distinct orange and cream colors, making a beautiful plate when served with a bright green vegetable as well. The peeling is an extra step that can't be avoided, but then the vegetables cook unattended. Just mash with a fork or hand-held potato masher right before serving.

Serves 4

4 large carrots

3 large parsnips

1 teaspoon salt

Freshly ground black pepper

1 Peel the carrots and parsnips and chop them into large chunks. Place the pieces in a large saucepan and add 2 inches of cold water.

2 Add salt and a few grindings of black pepper. Place over medium heat, cover, and leave to simmer for 15 minutes, or until vegetables are tender.

3 Mash with a fork or hand-held potato masher until coarsely combined. Add more salt and pepper if needed and serve.

YOU'LL THANK YOURSELF LATER

Make a double (or even triple) batch of mashed carrots and parsnips. They store especially well in the refrigerator and can be heated in the microwave, with no loss of flavor or texture, for meals throughout the week. You can even shape the cold mixture into little cakes, dust with flour, and lightly fry in butter for a special side dish.

Stir-Fried Romaine

When the only vegetable lurking in the fridge is a romaine lettuce, but you can't face another green salad, have your salad hot instead. Few cultures do so much, so imaginatively, with vegetables as the Chinese, and this dish is no exception. You can also use bok choy or Napa cabbage for this dish.

Serves 2

- 1 head romaine lettuce
- 2 tablespoons vegetable oil
- 1 teaspoon red chili flakes
- 1 teaspoon sugar
- 1 tablespoon cider vinegar
- 1/2 cup water
- 1 chicken stock cube

1. Cut off the root end of the romaine, about 1 inch up, so that the leaves are all separate.

2. Place a wok over high heat and add the vegetable oil. Swirl it to coat the sides of the pan. When the oil is hot, just starting to smoke, add the whole lettuce leaves and the chili flakes. Stir-fry quickly until the romaine starts to wilt, 30 seconds to 1 minute.

3. Add the remaining ingredients, breaking up the chicken stock cube, and stir until the liquid is boiling and the stock cube is incorporated. Serve immediately.

IF YOU'RE SO INCLINED

For another version of this dish with a thicker sauce, add 2 to 3 tablespoons of Chinese oyster sauce when you add the water and stock cube. Oyster sauce looks like dark ketchup, and has a faint oyster-like taste, though it doesn't actually contain oysters. Heat through and serve immediately.

Getting Time on Your Side

	The Old Way	The Lazy Way
Figuring out what vegetable side dishes to make	10 minutes	2 minutes
Making a pot of ratatouille	1 hour	15 minutes
Cooking a whole head of cauliflower	15 minutes (boiling)	7 minutes (steaming)
Creating an authentic tasting Chinese broccoli side dish	1 1/2 hours	7 minutes
Preparing Celeri Remoulade	1 hour	8 minutes
Preparing a big bowl of potato salad	4 hours	35 minutes

Sweetly Simple: Desserts

I completely support buying ready-made desserts for the lazy dinner table. Why should I spend all day trying to make and fill cannoli, when it will take me two minutes to pick some up at the Italian bakery up the street for a fraction of the cost? I make a point of buying nice desserts (chocolate truffle cakes, for example) when I serve them at (or take them to) a dinner party. But for casual family dinners, I'm not above picking up a half-price pound cake or angel food cake at the grocery store and serving it with ice cream.

Ah, ice cream! That's the real Lazy dessert. Those two gentlemen from Vermont are welcome in my home at any time, in any flavor. For lesser brands, you can always top them with sliced fruit or some commercial chocolate or butterscotch sauce. And if you have ice cream and chocolate on hand, then you only need bananas to have banana splits, which can be especially fun if you let everyone build their own at the table.

But those store-bought calories can add up more quickly than homemade, especially in the case of premium ice creams, whose butterfat contents equal the IQ of most people. Sometimes it's much easier and healthier to resort to fresh fruit—even with a bit of sugar and cream.

Fresh fruit is the friend of dessert-eaters in a hurry. There is always the elegant simplicity of a ripe pear, a wedge of Gorgonzola, and a small fruit knife; but if you want more substance (or more sugar), serve quick fruit crumbles or "Lazy Fool," a super-easy version of a British fruit dessert.

Cake mixes are not bad if you have to make a baked good with your own two hands, but I don't tend to stock those too often. I usually find it just as easy to make a "crazy cake," a one-dish affair with no eggs. It's very simple and people always say with delight, "You baked!" Well, yeah, kind of. At least I turned on the oven.

For those few times when I really need to pull out all the stops, I've devised a lazy procedure for making a wonderfully good lemon meringue pie that goes from frozen crust to beautifully browned meringue in, I swear, less than 20 minutes (it may take you five minutes more, until you get the technique down).

One of my personal favorites on my lazy shelf of fabulous desserts is something that may seem the very antithesis of lazy: crepes. The secret is mixing the batter in a blender and making very large crepes so each person only needs one. With the addition of a ready-made filling that I first met in Paris, the busy cook can create what I like to call "Paris Cafe in a Blender." It's the best kind of Lazy dessert. While your guests wolf it down, it lets you feel lazy *and* smug.

Campfire Banana Boats

Take chocolate and marshmallows, add a campfire, and you've probably got some fabulously sticky, melting dessert. S'mores, the classic of a toasted marshmallow squashed between two graham crackers with a square of chocolate, really require a campfire for the proper flavor, but banana boats can be successfully transferred to the kitchen.

We're going to bake these delectable little goodies, but you could also lay the foil packages on an outdoor grill. Or in the embers of a campfire while you sing "Kumbaya" in rounds.

Serves 4

4 ripe (but not brown) bananas, still in their peels
One 4-ounce bar milk chocolate
Mini-marshmallows

1. Preheat the oven to 350°. Slice the bananas down the middle lengthwise, without cutting through the peel on the opposite side.

2. Pack 1/4 of the chocolate bar and as many marshmallows as you can fit down the middle of each banana. Wrap tightly in foil.

3. Lay the foil packs on a baking sheet and place in the oven for 10 minutes, or until the chocolate and marshmallows are melted and gooey. Remove and serve a whole foil pack on a plate to catch drips, since you're not actually sitting outside by a fire.

QUICK 🔳 PAINLESS

It's a dessert; it's a kids' project. Don't make these yourself but call any little helpers you might have around the house to assemble the packages while you make dinner. (This works equally well even if your house is populated only by grown-ups.)

Macerated Fruit

This is really plain fruit that's gussied up a bit so your guests will know that you went to some effort. Macerating, or soaking, the fruit in sugar, liquor, and a bit of vanilla makes a heavenly fragrant juice that pools around the fruit.

The secret to easy fruit desserts lies in using fruits that don't require much effort on your part, and that usually means fresh berries. A quick rinse is all most of them need, although you do have to pull off the caps of strawberries. I cut the caps off, which may waste a bit but makes it move much faster than pinching them out with my thumbnail.

Although I call for Grand Marnier in this recipe, you can use any liquor or liqueur—a dash of cognac, some Drambuie or Amaretto, or a bit of dark rum. The orange zest is optional, but you can quickly grate it right off an orange that can then return to the fruit bowl.

Serve the macerated fruit plain or topped with unwhipped heavy cream, a frozen dessert topping, or some vanilla ice cream. A store-bought sugar cookie is a good accompaniment.

Serves 4

3 cups fresh berries (strawberries, blueberries, black-berries, raspberries)

3 tablespoons sugar

2 tablespoons Grand Marnier (or other liqueur)

1/2 teaspoon vanilla extract

1/2 teaspoon orange zest (optional)

YOU'LL THANK YOURSELF LATER

Try buying a combination of fresh berries for the best effect—raspberries and blackberries look nice together, or strawberries and blueberries. A few kiwis add a colorful touch and starfruit is decorative, if a bit flavorless. Peaches in season are lovely but may get a little mushy. Stay away from bananas, which get slimy if they're macerated.

1 Rinse the berries, drain well, and remove any stems or leaves.

2 Place them in a glass bowl and sprinkle with sugar, liqueur, vanilla, and orange zest if using. Mix lightly and very gently to keep from breaking up the berries. Macerate in the refrigerator for about 30 minutes.

QUICK n PAINLESS

Too tired even to macerate fruit? Here's a little novelty dessert that you won't want to serve to guests, but which makes a delightful end to a family dinner. Everyone slices one ripe banana lengthwise, sprinkles it with granulated sugar, and drizzles it with fresh lemon juice. Eat it with a spoon out of the skin. It's refreshingly simple and strangely delicious.

Lazy Fool

Fruit fools are a British dessert not often seen in the U.S. Gooseberry fool and rhubarb fool are particularly popular. They're made by cleaning and chopping the fruit, slowly stewing them with sugar, and then mashing them into a thick puree. This mixture is then gently folded into whipped cream, chilled, and the soft fruity mass is mounded into serving dishes. It's easy, but distinctly time-consuming.

I came up with Lazy Fool when, in need of a quick dessert, my fridge yielded nothing more than frozen raspberries and a carton of cream. Whipped cream on frozen berries doesn't look very exciting and the texture is mushy, but raspberries whizzed with sugar in the food processor or blender to form a puree, and then folded into whipped cream is another matter entirely.

You have to use a few dishes, but the result is still very quick and delicious. Pile it all into tall glasses for an elegant effect, and stick a finger of shortbread on top to be really frou-frou.

Serves 4

1 pound ripe berries (strawberries, raspberries, blueberries), or one 10-ounce package frozen berries

¼ cup sugar (or more to taste)

1 to 2 tablespoons Grand Marnier or orange juice (optional)

½ pint heavy whipping cream

1 teaspoon vanilla extract

IF YOU'RE SO *INCLINED*

You can also make fruit fools with other soft, fresh, sweet fruits such as mangos, nectarines, and peaches. Just peel, core, and pulse the fruit in a food processor with sugar, as instructed. Keep away from firm fruits such as apples, and citrus fruits, including kiwis, which tend to break down the cream.

1. Rinse the fresh berries, and remove any stems or leaves. (If you use frozen berries, nuke them for less than a minute. They can be still somewhat frozen, but it will soften them up a bit.)

2. In a food processor or blender, puree the berries with the sugar and Grand Marnier or juice until smooth. Taste and add more sugar if necessary.

3. Using beaters, whip the cream with the vanilla in a medium bowl until it forms stiff peaks.

4. Gently fold the fruit puree into the whipped cream and serve. If you want to make it in advance, it can be kept in the fridge for several hours, but it won't keep well overnight.

QUICK ☞ PAINLESS

It won't be authentic, but for an even Lazier Fool, skip the step where you puree the berries. Stir them directly into the whipped cream, along with the sugar, Grand Marnier, and vanilla, and mound into serving dishes.

Fruit Crumble

There may come a day when you have to turn on the oven and bake something for dessert, and Fruit Crumble is the answer. You can do a little work and use up those old apples browning in your fruit bowl, or you can do the really lazy thing and open some canned peaches or pears. Use your judgment and increase the sugar on the fresh fruit if you like, especially if you know the plums you're using are particularly tart.

A quick topping of butter, brown sugar, and rolled oats, 25 minutes in the oven, and you have a hot dessert. The canned fruit kind is ideal for those winter evenings when you've long since finished dinner and done the dishes, and still your spouse is cruising through the kitchen, wondering aloud "Isn't there something sweet to eat?"

Serves 4

1 1/2 pounds fresh fruit (such as apples, plums, apricots, pears, or peaches), or two 28-ounce cans of fruit in light syrup (such as peaches or pears)

1/2 lemon

1/4 cup sugar

For topping

1/2 cup (1 stick) unsalted butter

3/4 cup rolled oats

3/4 cup brown sugar

2 tablespoons all-purpose flour

1 teaspoon cinnamon

1 Preheat the oven to 350°. Butter a small 1-quart baking dish.

2 If using canned fruit, go to step 4. If you use fresh fruit, core or seed it, and cut it into small chunks directly into the baking dish.

3 Hold a strainer over the baking dish and squeeze the juice from the half lemon over the fruit. Sprinkle the sugar over the fruit.

4 If you use canned fruit, drain it, retaining a few table-spoons of juice for moisture, and dump the fruit and reserved juice into the baking dish. Use a knife to cut it into small chunks.

5 In the food processor or in a small bowl, combine the topping ingredients. Pulse in the processor, or mix with a fork or your fingers, until the butter is absorbed and the mixture is crumbly.

6 Sprinkle over the fruit, and bake for about 30 minutes for fresh fruit or 20 minutes for canned fruit.

IF YOU'RE SO
INCLINED

Instead of a crumble top-ping, you can make this into a crustless fruit pie. Buy ready-rolled pie crust in the refrigerator sec-tion. Spread the fruit into a round glass pie dish and sprinkle with sugar and lemon. Lay the round pie crust on top, cut a few slits into it with a knife, and sprinkle with sugar and cinnamon. Bake as directed, until crust is golden brown and fruit is bubbling.

Super-Quick Mexican Chocolate Cake

Mix it and bake it, even eat it if you like, all in one 8 x 8-inch glass pan. It's so fast you don't even have to slow down to crack an egg; and the only pieces of equipment you need are the pan, an oven, and a fork.

There are several variations of this type of one-pan cake, but my Mexican version has a zesty addition of cinnamon to give it extra interest. You can add other ingredients that you may have in your pantry, such as 1/2 cup of chocolate chips or some chopped nuts.

Serves 9

Dry ingredients

1 1/4 cups all-purpose flour

1 cup sugar

1/2 cup unsweetened cocoa

1 1/2 teaspoons cinnamon

1 teaspoon baking soda

1/2 teaspoon salt

Wet ingredients

1 cup water

1 teaspoon vanilla extract

1/3 cup vegetable oil

1 teaspoon white vinegar

IF YOU'RE SO INCLINED

You can whip up an easy frosting by blending half a stick (4 tablespoons) of softened butter with 1 cup of powdered sugar and 1/4 cup of unsweetened cocoa. If the frosting is too thick, add a teaspoon of milk. Wait until the cake is completely cooled before you spread on the frosting.

1 Preheat oven to 350°. Place all dry ingredients in an 8 × 8-inch glass baking dish and combine them with a fork.

2 Using the fork, make a well in the center of the dry ingredients. Pour in all the wet ingredients and stir well with the fork, making sure to scrape the dry ingredients up from the corners.

3 Put the cake in the oven and bake for 25 to 30 minutes, until a knife inserted in the center comes out clean (or you can poke it with that fork). Remove it and let it cool for at least half an hour.

YOU'LL THANK YOURSELF LATER

If you go to eat this cake the day after you've made it, you'll notice that the chocolate taste has bloomed, but the cake is somewhat drier. Serve squares of cake with fresh fruit and ice cream or a splash of canned chocolate sauce, heated for a minute in a cup in the microwave.

YOU'LL THANK YOURSELF LATER

Poach a few extra pears. They can move from dessert to salad with surprising ease: Serve them one night sliced and fanned over a bed of mesclun and garnished with slices of Gorgonzola. Store the rest in the refrigerator, and, later in the week, treat yourself to Poires Belle Helene for dessert: Place a scoop of vanilla ice cream in each individual serving bowl. Lay a poached pear on top and drizzle with store-bought chocolate sauce, heated first in the microwave if you like.

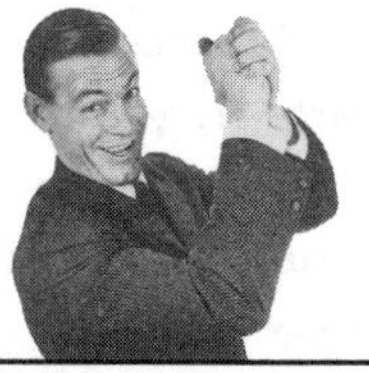

Poached Pears

Poached pears never stir my imagination until I make them, which usually happens when I notice that I have the ingredients. Then I always wonder why I don't make them more often. The lightly spicy, wine-y fragrance that rises from the pan while the pears simmer is heavenly. They taste marvelous served alone or with a trickle of cream; even better with a dollop of vanilla ice cream or frozen yogurt to melt into the light syrup.

You can use pears at any stage of ripeness. If they're quite firm, cook them longer, until tender; if they're overripe, reduce the cooking time to keep them from turning into mush. In a fancy restaurant, the pears are peeled before poaching, but I confess to often poaching them in their skins. Instead of feeling inadequate, I congratulate myself on getting a little extra fiber.

Serves 4

4 large ripe pears (I like Bartlett or Bosc)
2 cups red wine
2 cups water
1 cup sugar
2 cinnamon sticks
1 lemon (optional)

1 If you want to, peel the pears, leaving the stems on.

2 In a large saucepan, combine the wine, water, sugar, and cinnamon sticks. If you want to add lemon zest, use a small knife or vegetable peeler to peel the zest off the lemon in one long strip, and drop it into the liquid.

3 Stir the syrup to combine and heat over medium-high heat until the sugar is dissolved.

4 Bring to a boil, add the pears, and reduce the heat. Cover the pan loosely and simmer until the pears are tender, turning them occasionally in the liquid. Ripe pears should be tender in 10 to 15 minutes.

5 Serve warm right away or let the pears cool in the syrup. Store the pears, in the syrup, in the refrigerator.

QUICK in PAINLESS

It's not poaching, but you can cook pears in the microwave to the same softness as poaching. Place 2 unpeeled pears on a shallow glass, microwavable dish. Pierce the skin of each several times with a sharp knife. Cook on high for 5 to 7 minutes or until pears are tender.

Lazy Lemon Meringue

Any dish that includes a cooked filling and a meringue top-ping may not seem very lazy, but this pie is my secret weapon when I have to make a real dessert—to take to some event, say, or for a special guest. The secret is to do everything all at once and in less than 20 minutes. While the ready-made frozen crust bakes, you make the hot filling and whip the egg whites. Instead of waiting for both to cool, the hot filling goes immediately into the hot crust, the meringue is spread on top, and pie is put back into the same hot oven to brown.

As long as both crust and filling are hot, the crust won't get soggy. But if the crust cools, the filling must as well, and that's what slows you down.

Makes one 9-inch pie, to serve 6

One 9-inch ready-made pie crust (preferably deep dish)
4 large eggs
2 lemons
1^1/2 cups sugar
^{1}/4 cup cornstarch
1^1/2 cups water
2 tablespoons unsalted butter
^{1}/4 teaspoon cream of tartar

1 Preheat the oven to 350°. (The crust's package may say 400, but you're buying a bit of time for yourself.)

2 Separate the eggs, putting the whites in a clean mixing bowl and the yolks in a small cup.

3 Grate the zest off the lemons and set it aside, and then juice the lemons and set aside.

A COMPLETE WASTE OF TIME

The 3 Worst Things to Do with Meringue:

1. **Get any egg yolk in with the whites.**

2. **Allow any filling to show between the meringue and the crust.**

3. **Store it in the refrigerator.**

4 Prick the pie crust in several places with a fork and put it in the oven to bake for about 15 minutes. (Now your clock is ticking.)

5 In a small saucepan, place 1 cup of the sugar and the cornstarch and mix together with a whisk. Heat the pan over medium-high heat and slowly stir in the water, using a whisk. Bring the mixture to a boil, whisking all the time. Let it bubble for several minutes, until it's thick and smooth.

6 Using the whisk, blend some of the hot mixture into the egg yolks, and then whisk it back into the cornstarch mixture. Cook, whisking constantly, for several minutes until it's thick and smooth. Add the lemon juice, zest, and butter, and remove it from the heat.

7 Check the pie crust. It should still have several minutes to bake, so quickly make the meringue. (If the crust is already too dark, remove it from the oven, spoon in the filling, and then let it sit while you make the meringue.) Using beaters, whip the egg whites with the cream of tartar until they form soft peaks; keep beating them while adding the remaining 1/2 cup sugar, a little at a time, until the mixture forms firm peaks.

8 Take the pie crust out of the oven, spoon the hot filling into it, and smooth the meringue over the top. Use the back of the spoon to make little peaks on top, if you like, then put the pie in the hot oven for about 5 minutes until the meringue is lightly browned. Remove and allow to cool.

QUICK 🔲 PAINLESS

The fastest way to grate zest off of fruit is to use a zester—a hand-held tool that has small holes at one end and a larger hole at the other. Just hold the zester snugly against the fruit and pull as if you're peeling it. If you really can't face grating the zest off the lemons, leave the zest out and add 1 teaspoon of lemon flavoring along with the lemon juice.

Paris Cafe in a Blender
(or, Nutella Crepes)

On a rainy afternoon in a Paris cafe, I watched an elderly woman make crepe after crepe, to be eaten in the cafe or sold through a little window to passersby. The filling of choice was Nutella, the hazelnut-chocolate paste that Europeans eat the way Americans eat peanut butter. She slathered on a thin layer of Nutella, folded the crepe in four, and the chocolate filling melted into creamy splendor.

Crepes fit the busy cook's lifestyle surprisingly well, I'm very pleased to say. With your crepe batter quickly whirred into a thick cream in a blender, and a large, hot nonstick pan nearby to make the big pancakes, you can have Nutella crepes for four in less than 10 minutes. The batter makes a more tender crepe after it rests for an hour or so, so you might mix it before dinner and let it sit. You can also store it in the refrigerator and make a crepe or two throughout the week.

Makes about ten 12-inch crepes

1 cup milk

3 large eggs

3 tablespoons melted unsalted butter (or vegetable oil)

1 cup all-purpose flour

1/4 cup sugar

Pinch of salt

Butter for cooking crepes

Nutella

You've actually made fabulous French crepes. Make yourself a cup of espresso with sugar (the French way), and pretend you're in a Paris cafe while you eat. (Remember to be very rude to yourself when you try to order!)

The Lazy Way

1 Put the milk and eggs in the blender first. Melt the butter in a cup in the microwave and add it to the blender (or use vegetable oil and skip the microwave).

2 Add flour, sugar, and salt to the blender. Blend until smooth and creamy. Let the batter rest for about an hour, if possible.

3 Heat a 12-inch nonstick skillet over medium heat. Put about a teaspoon of butter in the pan and tip the pan to spread it around. When melted and sizzling but not browned (if it browns, wipe it out with a paper towel and start again), add a scant 1/3 cup of crepe batter and tilt the pan to spread. You want a very thin coating, as wide as the pan.

4 When the underside has browned and the edges curl slightly (in about a minute or so), use a spatula or tongs to turn the crepe over, and cook another few seconds to lightly brown the other side.

5 If you're making several crepes, stack them on a paper towel-lined plate on the stove. If your Nutella is very firm, soften some slightly in the microwave. When you're ready to serve (the crepes should still be hot), use a wide knife to slather a good dollop of Nutella thinly across the whole crepe. Fold in half, then in half again.

YOU'LL THANK YOURSELF LATER

Freeze extra crepes by stacking them with layers of waxed paper in between. Thaw as many as needed for a few seconds in the microwave, and slather on your filling.

Food Processor Clafouti

A clafouti is a French fruit pudding, traditionally made with fresh cherries that haven't been stoned, so that individual diners have to spit out the pits as they eat. I find that to be a marvelous tribute to a streak of convenience for the cook in French cuisine, and it has inspired me to take clafouti a step further and make it even easier for the cook.

Serves 4 to 6

1 pound soft fresh fruit, such as apricots, plums, peaches, nectarines, very ripe pears, etc.

2 tablespoons brown sugar

2 large eggs

1 1/2 cups milk

1/2 cup all-purpose flour

1/2 cup sugar

1 teaspoon vanilla

1/4 teaspoon nutmeg

1. Preheat the oven to 350°. Prepare the fruit by pitting, halving, or slicing (no need to peel them unless you're using fuzzy peaches), and place in a small (6-cup) casserole or baking dish. Sprinkle the brown sugar over the fruit.

2. Put the remaining ingredients in the food processor or blender in the order given. Pulse briefly until the mixture is well-blended and frothy.

3. Pour the clafouti batter over the fruit. Bake it for 30 to 35 minutes until the top is puffed and golden, and the pudding is set. Serve it while it's still warm.

Gingerbread

Not gingerbread cookies, but a trayful of fragrant cake-like gingerbread, the kind that fills the whole kitchen with aromas of spices and molasses. Extra ginger makes this version particularly flavorful and spicy. It's the kind of comforting dessert you'll want to have with a glass of milk at the kitchen table.

Usually it takes several steps to mix this really moist batter, including melting the butter and molasses together on top of the stove. But with the help of a food processor to mix the batter, you can be baking in minutes. Put it in the oven before you eat, and it will be ready shortly after dinner.

Serves 9

1/2 cup (1 stick) butter or margarine, softened

1/2 cup brown sugar

2 large eggs

1/2 cup milk

1 cup molasses

2 cups flour

1 tablespoon ground ginger

1 teaspoon baking soda

1 Preheat the oven to 350°. Spray-grease a 9 × 9- or 8 × 8-inch glass or metal baking dish.

2 Place the softened butter and the brown sugar in the food processor and pulse for a few seconds to combine. Add the eggs, milk, and molasses, and process until smooth.

3 Add the remaining ingredients and process until smooth. Pour the batter into the prepared baking dish and bake for 1 hour, until a knife inserted in center comes out clean.

YOU'LL THANK YOURSELF LATER

If there's any gingerbread left over, you'll find that the ginger taste will be more pronounced the next day but the cake may be somewhat drier. To liven up the gingerbread, heat leftover squares on a plate for a minute in the microwave, and serve them with fruit and ice cream. (Try it with sliced peaches and vanilla ice cream.)

This pudding is delicious alone, but for a really festive treat, heat some butterscotch ice cream topping in a small cup in the microwave and drizzle it over each serving.

Busy Bread-and-Butter Pudding

The bread for bread pudding can be left whole instead of broken into pieces, and it's improved by a thin slather of butter on each slice before it's layered in the baking dish. In this speedy recipe, the egg and milk is mixed in the baking dish and the bread is pushed down into it, thereby using only one dish for preparation.

You can make an edible pudding with white sandwich bread, but it'll taste much better if you have a good white bakery bread, and even better if you use a cake-like egg or potato bread.

Serves 4

2^1/$_2$ cups milk

2 large eggs

^{1}/$_4$ cup sugar

^{1}/$_2$ teaspoon vanilla

4 slices white bread

Butter

^{1}/$_4$ cup raisins

1 Preheat the oven to 350°. In a small (6-cup) baking dish, place the milk, eggs, sugar, and vanilla. Beat lightly with a fork or whisk until eggs are incorporated.

2 Spread each slice of bread with a thin layer of butter. Lay the bread in the milk mixture, tearing if needed to make it fit.

3 Sprinkle the raisins over all and bake for 45 minutes, until puffed and golden.

Shortcut Shortbread

Cookies aren't usually on the repertoire of cooks in a hurry, but if you need to bake some, shortbread is just the ticket. Besides the fact that it's baked all in one piece (no shaping or dropping individual cookies), you can mix this version in a food processor.

Traditional Scottish shortbread includes rice flour, which gives it the faintly nubbly texture. Since most of us don't keep a lot of ground rice on hand, you can use some cornstarch instead with quite good results.

Serves 8

1 cup flour

¹/₄ cup cornstarch

¹/₄ cup sugar

¹/₂ cup (1 stick) butter, softened

1 Preheat oven to 350°. Place the ingredients, in the order listed, in the work bowl of the food processor.

2 Pulse until the ingredients hold loosely in the shape of a ball. (You may have to stop the machine and use a knife to help break up the butter.) Drop the dough onto a clean, ungreased baking sheet, and knead a couple of strokes to make any loose crumbs adhere.

3 Use your fingers to press the dough out into a circle about 7 inches in diameter. Prick with a fork to make the dotted outlines of 8 pie-shaped wedges, as if cutting a pizza.

4 Bake for 30 minutes, until still pale but starting to turn golden. Cool and break along perforations.

YOU'LL THANK YOURSELF LATER

Bake extra rounds of shortbread to store tightly sealed in tins to serve with ice cream for a simple dessert. Or, use two whole rounds for a different and impromptu strawberry shortcake. Spoon sliced berries onto one round, then cover with whipped cream. Lay the second round on top and cover with more strawberries and cream.

Getting Time on Your Side

	The Old Way	The Lazy Way
Mixing a batch of moist and fragrant gingerbread	25 minutes	5 minutes
Assembling and baking a tray of bread pudding	1 1/2 hours	35 minutes
Making the dough for Scottish shortbread	15 minutes	3 minutes
Preparing the batter and fruit for a French clafouti	45 minutes	8 minutes
Making a show-stopping lemon meringue pie	3 hours	20 minutes
Whipping up a home-baked chocolate cake	1 1/2 hours	35 minutes

Chapter

sixteen

The Quickest Quick Breads

Baking and the lazy kitchen don't have to be utter strangers, but it's true that they're not intimate acquaintances. Unlike the sweet breakfast breads in Chapter 6, designed to provide breakfast for a work week, these savory breads are made to accompany a specific meal and won't hold up for much longer.

Because of that, these quick breads are probably best saved for one of those nights when you're not doing a lot of other cooking, such as when you've bought a rotisserie chicken, you're heating up a jar of store-bought spaghetti sauce to serve on angel hair pasta, or you're preparing to eat a one-pot stew that's been simmering in the slow cooker all day. Pop one of these super-quick and savory breads in the oven as an accompaniment, and the whole kitchen will smell of fragrant, home-cooked food.

Quick breads rise as a result of leaveners that raise the bread with air released from chemical interaction. The leavener can be eggs, baking powder, or a combination of an acid and a base, such as yogurt or buttermilk, and baking soda. When all your ingredients have been combined, you want to get the batter into the oven as swiftly as possible to take advantage of all that chemical interaction to raise the bread, and the food processor is a great way to speed the mixing.

All the recipes that follow can be mixed in the food processor. So turn on the oven, pulse the batter in the machine, and spoon it into a spray-greased loaf pan or paper-lined muffin cups. By the time it's baked, in as little as 10 minutes but no longer than 30 for any of these recipes, the rest of dinner will be ready. You'll have no problem assembling everyone at the table when they get a sniff of that hot bread.

Be extra careful not to overprocess any of these delicate breads or you'll end up with a tough, inedible product. The more you process a quick bread such as the Yogurt Dill Muffins, the more you'll develop the gluten, which is the protein in the flour. While that's great for making extra-chewy French baguettes, it's the toll of doom for a tender muffin. When it comes to combining wet and dry ingredients for these breads, err on the side of undermixed rather than overmixed. Don't try to get them smooth. It's okay, it's even preferable, to have a few lumps in the batter.

Yogurt Dill Muffins

A fragrant muffin with a tender crumb and a slightly tangy flavor, this hereby delight is a perfect accompaniment to a stew or soup. You can vary the herb used to suit the food you're serving it with: try rosemary, oregano, fresh chives, or simply parsley. Make extra-sure not to overbeat these in the food processor or they'll be extremely tough or even inedible.

Makes 12 muffins

> 2 large eggs
> 1 cup plain yogurt
> 1/2 cup vegetable oil

Dry ingredients

> 2 cups all-purpose flour
> 2 teaspoons baking powder
> 1 teaspoon sugar
> 1/2 teaspoon baking soda
> 1 teaspoon salt
> 2 teaspoons dried dill, or 2 tablespoons fresh dill

1 Preheat the oven to 400° and place paper liners in 12 muffin cups.

2 In the food processor, pulse the eggs, yogurt, and oil until well blended. Add the dry ingredients and pulse as briefly as possible until the ingredients are just moistened and still lumpy. (Pulse for 3 seconds and check, then again if necessary.)

3 Spoon the batter into the muffin cups and bake for 12 to 15 minutes until the tops are puffed and golden. Eat them right away—they don't last well overnight.

A COMPLETE WASTE OF TIME

The 3 Worst Things to Do with Delicate Herb Muffins:

1. Overmix them so they bake up too tough to eat.

2. Not eat them while they're fresh and moist.

3. Use stale dried herbs which deprive them of flavor and scent.

Jalapeño Corn Muffins

Hearty corn muffins are even more versatile than tender white muffins because sturdy cornmeal can take on even stronger flavors, such as chilis and cheese, and more solid ingredients, such as corn kernels and chopped green pepper. This recipe uses pickled jalapeños (like the kind you get on nachos). You can substitute a small can of milder diced green chilis, drained.

And I must confess that these muffins are made Southern style, which is never sweet. Sugar in your cornbread is considered anathema in the South, where cornbread should be moist, grainy, and savory. If you think cornbreads of any sort taste funny without sugar, try the cornbread recipe that follows this one.

Makes 10 muffins

2 large eggs
1 cup buttermilk
1/4 cup vegetable oil or butter (1/2 stick)
1 to 2 pickled jalapeños

Dry ingredients

1 1/2 cups yellow cornmeal (preferably stone-ground)
1/4 cup all-purpose flour
2 teaspoons baking powder
1/2 teaspoon baking soda
1/2 teaspoon salt

IF YOU'RE SO INCLINED

Variations:

Spicy: Add 1/2 teaspoon ground cumin when you add the dry ingredients.

Chili-Cheese: Add 1/2 cup grated Cheddar when you add the dry ingredients.

Corn: Add one 14-ounce can drained corn when you add the dry ingredients.

1 Preheat the oven to 425°. Place paper liners in 10 muffin cups.

2 In the work bowl of a food processor, place the eggs, buttermilk, and oil. (If you use butter, melt it in a small cup in the microwave first.)

3 Take the stems off the pickled jalapeños, and scrape out and discard the seeds. Put the jalapeños in the food processor and pulse until the liquids are well combined and the jalapeños are finely chopped, but not pureed.

4 Add the dry ingredients and pulse very briefly, until the ingredients are just combined.

5 Spoon the batter into the muffin cups and bake for 15 to 20 minutes, until golden brown. Eat right away.

YOU'LL THANK YOURSELF LATER

Moist corn muffins are a good bet for freezing. Make a double batch and freeze half in a zipperlock plastic bag. Microwave briefly to thaw and heat.

QUICK n' PAINLESS

Yeast bread is also a possibility for the lazy kitchen, but take the shortcut and buy frozen bread dough, available in the freezer section of most supermarkets. As this dough thaws, the yeast starts to work. You can shape it into loaves, buns, or even dinner rolls (put three knobs of dough in a greased muffin cup), and the result tastes as good as if you'd been up since dawn mixing the yeast dough yourself.

Cornbread

This is a sweet, light cornbread, the kind that Southerners tend to dismiss as "Yankee cornbread." The light texture lends itself to sweeter additions, and the following recipe also makes terrific muffins, especially if you add 1 cup of fresh or frozen blueberries.

Makes One 8 × 8-inch loaf

2 large eggs
$1/2$ cup vegetable oil
1 cup buttermilk

Dry ingredients

$1^1/2$ cups all-purpose flour
$1/2$ cup yellow cornmeal (preferably stoneground)
$1/4$ cup sugar
2 teaspoons baking powder
$1/2$ teaspoon baking soda
$1/2$ teaspoon salt

1 Preheat the oven to 450°. Lightly spray an 8 x 8-inch pan with cooking spray.

2 In the work bowl of a food processor, place the eggs, oil, and buttermilk, and pulse to combine.

3 Add the dry ingredients and pulse briefly until just combined and until all the dry ingredients are moistened but the mixture is still slightly lumpy.

4 Pour the batter into the prepared pan and bake for 20 to 25 minutes, until golden brown. Cut into 9 squares and serve with butter.

Buttermilk Drop Biscuits

Because hot biscuits at nearly every meal are regarded by many Southerners as a birthright, many Southern ladies of a certain age can mix, roll, cut, and bake a tray of biscuits in their sleep. It's not quite so easy if you didn't start around the age of six, but I find that this food processor-mixed, spoon-dropped version creates a reasonable facsimile. If you don't have buttermilk, you can substitute 3/4 cup plain yogurt, thinned with 1/4 cup milk.

Makes 10 to 12 biscuits

> 2 cups all-purpose flour
> 2 teaspoons baking powder
> 1/2 teaspoon baking soda
> 1/4 teaspoon salt
> 6 tablespoons butter, shortening, or margarine
> 1 cup buttermilk

1. Preheat the oven to 425°.

2. In the work bowl of a food processor, place the flour, baking powder, baking soda, and salt. Pulse once to combine.

3. Add the butter or shortening in pieces, not in one big lump. Pulse on and off for a few seconds until the mixture makes coarse crumbs. Pour in the buttermilk all at once and pulse just enough to moisten. Do not overmix. The dough should be soft, lumpy, and wet-looking.

4. Drop big spoonfuls of dough onto an ungreased baking sheet. Bake for 10 to 15 minutes, until raised and golden brown. Serve immediately.

Wow! You made piping-hot, flaky buttermilk biscuits to rival those of any Southern grandma. Put on your favorite Country & Western CD and have a bit of a hoe-down after dinner.

The Lazy Way

When scraping the dough out onto a floured surface to shape it into rolls, first lay down a large sheet of waxed paper and sprinkle flour over it. Put the dough on the floured paper and shape it. When you're done, crumple up the waxed paper and throw it away. The counter is clean!

No-Rise Oatmeal Yeast Rolls

This is a soft yeast dough that requires no rise and results in a very tender bread. It doesn't work very well in a loaf pan because of the lack of rising, but it makes excellent dinner rolls. The heat of the oven makes the little rolls rise just enough—they won't be as light as fully risen rolls, but they're still delicious served warm and slathered with butter. Let them cool a bit before you slice them open and butter them or they'll deflate.

This bread is a little bit more work because you have to divide the dough into balls by hand, but it's the fastest way I know to make homemade yeast bread.

Makes 10 rolls

1 cup warm water (not boiling, but hot from the tap, which is usually about 110°)

1 package yeast

1 teaspoon sugar

1 tablespoon vegetable oil

1 teaspoon salt

2 1/2 cups all-purpose flour

1/4 cup rolled oats

1 Preheat the oven to 400°.

2 In the work bowl of the food processor, place the hot tap water and sprinkle the yeast over it. Add the sugar and leave it for 5 minutes until the yeast is fully dissolved and slightly foamy.

3 Add the remaining ingredients and pulse to form a soft dough. Scrape the dough out onto a floured surface, dip your hands in flour, and roll the dough into a cylinder about 18 inches long. Cut it into 10 pieces and lightly roll each into a ball.

4 Lay the rolls on an ungreased baking sheet and bake them for 15 to 20 minutes until risen and browned. Remove the rolls from the oven and let them cool for about 10 minutes before eating. If you cut into them when piping hot, they'll be too doughy.

QUICK n' PAINLESS

Don't be a slave to yeast. If you do make a yeast-raised bread, adapt the recipe to *your* schedule. The dough can be mixed and left to rise overnight in the refrigerator, or even left there for several days. The cold doesn't kill the yeast, it just slows it down, and the bread continues to rise. When you're ready to bake, remove the dough from the fridge, punch it down, and let it rise again another 30 to 45 minutes, then bake. An added benefit to subduing yeast to your schedule is that very slowly raised bread develops a much better flavor.

Getting Time on Your Side

	The Old Way	The Lazy Way
Whipping up a pan of muffins—and cleaning the baking tin	1 hour	15 minutes
Mixing batter for corn muffins packed with extra ingredients such as cheese and chilis	10 minutes	2 minutes
Rising time for a loaf of oatmeal yeast bread	1 hour	0 minutes
Cleaning the countertop after kneading bread	10 minutes	0 minutes
Making yeast-raised rolls or buns	4 hours	1 hour (frozen dough!)
Getting your family to come to the dinner table when you call	5 to 10 minutes	30 seconds

Hassle-Free Holidays and Entertaining

Most holidays and parties are all about food, so if you don't like to spend whole days in the kitchen, it doesn't seem like much cause for celebration. But cheer up! There are ways to make the holidays more fun and much easier, as well as ways to make entertaining less of a chore. When you have guests to your home, your place is with them, not in front of the stove.

Certainly, one of the primary ways to lighten up the holidays is to buy some of the food already cooked. During the holidays, this isn't a problem because most stores bring out their best. Your job is take advantage of it without putting an obviously store-bought meal on the table. Although it is acceptable to serve an entirely purchased meal, when guests come to our homes, either for dinner parties or to celebrate holidays or events, they like to feel that we went to some trouble to cook something and make them feel welcome. In addition, you want the house to smell of good food when you open the door to greet your guests.

Buy some things, make others, and don't be shy when guests ask, "Can I bring something?" The answer is yes! And you don't have to leave the choice to them. Have a menu in mind when you make the invitations. You needn't assign food to guests (that's called potluck, and for good reason), but if they offer to bring something, they mean it, and it's perfectly fine to say, "Why, Bob, I'm so glad you asked. I'd love it if you brought some of those fabulous brownies of yours. I was just thinking about them the other day." Which you were, of course, as you planned Bob's brownies with a scoop of vanilla ice cream for dessert (and if Bob should fail you, your well-stocked pantry will yield frozen raspberries to spoon over the ice cream instead).

The biggest part of most holiday meals is the cut of meat—such as the Christmas or Thanksgiving turkey—and the dessert, be it pumpkin or mince pie, or jack-o'-lantern-shaped cookies at Halloween. Happily, most grocery store delis will now prepare these for you.

A spiral-cut ham is a perfect example of a ready-made holiday food that saves you loads of time and energy. With judicious assistance from relatives and friends (let someone bring sweet potatoes, someone else bring green beans and bread, and another bring pie or cake), you may have little left to prepare except the beverages, salad, and mashed potatoes (make scalloped potatoes instead and all you have to do is peel, slice them in the food processor, and bake).

When guests come for a non-holiday dinner party, whether it be a casual meal or more formal entertaining, follow the same formula of serving some homemade dishes augmented by some store-bought foods (which you'll garnish to look more homemade where possible). The following menus and recipes are suggestions to help turn your mind toward the lazy method of entertaining. Having guests to your home should be pleasant for both you and them, and most parties go with an easy swing as long as there's a relaxed host and plenty of food. If you regularly knit up your insides in knots over entertaining, try one lazy party using these menus, and you may discover a whole new lease on party life!

The following are suggestions for traditional holiday menus that let the cook celebrate with the least amount of difficulty, using a combination of store-bought prepared foods and a few homemade things. It's perfectly acceptable to buy all the food and put it in your own serving dishes, but there are quick and easy recipes and suggestions in case you feel obliged to make some of it yourself.

FOURTH OF JULY

The Fourth of July almost always means a cookout, and fortunately we all have the menu practically engraved on our brains. Go the simple route, though—don't joint a chicken when you can open a package of hot dogs.

- Hamburgers and Hot Dogs on the Grill
- Fixings Platter
- Baked Beans
- Potato Salad
- Ice Cream Cake

Hamburgers and Hot Dogs on the Grill: A package of hamburger, slapped into patties as they go on the grill, and some hot dogs are the easiest things to barbecue for a crowd.

Fixings Platter: A fixings platter for the grilled meat should include buns, some sliced tomato and onion, lettuce, condiments such as relish, pickles, perhaps a dollop of store-bought coleslaw and a few slices of cheese—and not necessarily on one plate. Set the mustard and ketchup containers directly on the table instead of decanting them into little bowls.

Baked Beans: Baked beans are the traditional cook-out accompaniment, and that's probably because they're so easy. Open a large can of baked beans. Heat and serve. You can also take the time to doctor them up by pouring them into a baking dish and stirring in ketchup, molasses or brown sugar, and a dash of yellow mustard. Lay a few

QUICK IN PAINLESS

Decorating for this holiday is easy: simply buy blue paper plates, red plastic cups, and white napkins. And if you happen to see little American flags during your shop, buy a few and stick them in a vase (even a tin can with the label peeled off) for a centerpiece.

slices of bacon over the top and bake at 350° for about 30 minutes, until bubbling.

Potato Salad: Potato salad can be bought at a deli, or make the Lazy Potato Salad on page 224.

Ice Cream Cake: Ice cream cake rounds out a summer party particularly well. Happily, they're almost always tastier when store-bought. Alternately, set out bowls, a container of vanilla ice cream, a bunch of bananas, a jar of chocolate syrup, and some chopped nuts, and invite everyone to make their own sundae.

IF YOU'RE SO
INCLINED

If hot dogs have become too boring for you to serve them at one more barbecue, try grilling a combination of spicy and sweet Italian sausages. Instead of hot dog buns, serve them on baguettes that have been cut into 5- to 6-inch lengths and then sliced open. Slather with spicy brown mustard.

HALLOWEEN PARTY

Make simple food look fun for Halloween parties to entertain little ghosts and goblins. Children love gross and scary things like a few peeled grapes masquerading as eyeballs—and adults expect it with patient resignation and will avert their eyes. Decorate the table with dishes of instant vanilla pudding colored dark green for slime and put Vienna sausages in ketchup for bloody fingers. Make the food you actually plan to eat simple and quick.

- Pigs-in-Blankets
- Potato Chips
- Carrot Sticks and Halloween Hummus
- Pumpkin Sugar Cookies
- Mulled Cider

Pigs-in-Blankets: Pigs-in-Blankets may not be very elegant but they're eternally popular, especially among children, for a Halloween party. Buy small cocktail weinies and cans of biscuit dough, wrap each weinie in a biscuit, and bake at 350° for 15 to 20 minutes until the biscuits are puffed and golden. Serve with a bowl of commercially prepared honey-mustard sauce and a bowl of ketchup for dipping.

Potato Chips: Potato chips, corn chips, or some such crunchy items are necessary for this kind of party. Buy a very big bag, and dump all the chips into a large salad bowl or tureen for serving.

YOU'LL THANK YOURSELF LATER

Prepare the Pigs-in-Blankets up to a month in advance of your Halloween party. Wrap the biscuits around the cocktail weinies, lay them on a baking sheet or two, and freeze. When they're frozen (in 4 or 5 hours), place them in zipperlock plastic bags and seal. Bake them directly from the freezer for the party. Lay them on baking sheets and bake in a preheated 350° oven for about 25 minutes, until golden and puffed.

Carrot Sticks and Halloween Hummus: A vegetable of some sort is in order for any food event, and carrot sticks fit the bill for a kids' party. Serve on a platter with a bowl of store-bought hummus in the middle, and dot the platter with black olives—call it fingers and eyes for a Halloween theme. If you like, stir a drop or two of red food coloring into the hummus to give it an orange hue.

Pumpkin Sugar Cookies: A seasonally shaped cookie, such as orange-hued pumpkin sugar cookies, can usually be bought at any supermarket bakery in October. You can also buy packaged rolls of sugar cookie dough that you can roll and cut into pumpkin shapes, or buy the kind of dough that has a pumpkin face running through the roll. Simply slice and bake.

Mulled Cider: A special party beverage, such as mulled cider, helps to perfume the room and finishes off the menu with a homemade food. To serve 10, pour a gallon of cider into a large stockpot and add 1 cup of water, 3 cinnamon sticks, and an orange that is cut into quarters and stuck with 10 cloves. Simmer for about 40 minutes, until heated through and fragrant.

A COMPLETE WASTE OF TIME

The 3 Worst Things to Do When Entertaining:

1. Cook everything yourself so you're exhausted when the guests arrive.

2. Say "No" when guests ask if they can bring anything.

3. Apologize for anything that you serve, whether you made it or bought it.

A CHRISTMAS PARTY

You may be able to get out of hosting the big family Christmas dinner by having the crowd over on Christmas Eve for a bit of carol-singing and nibbles. Serve finger food, including the following hot dip, to show that you care.

As for decorating, dim the lights, turn on the tree, and light lots of candles. It not only makes the house looks festive but it hides the fact that you didn't have time to dust or tidy too much. When you're serving them good food at a nice party, nobody will care.

- Easy Eggnog
- Mulled Wine
- Cheese Ball and Crackers
- Hot Spinach Dip with Tortilla Chips or Rye Bread
- Store-bought Pastries, Cookies, Cakes

Easy Eggnog: Buy good quality, commercially prepared eggnog (the kind in the refrigerator section, not in a can), and spike it with brandy (or rum flavoring) and a hint of extra vanilla and nutmeg.

Mulled Wine: Simmer a couple of bottles of red wine on the back of the stove in a stockpot, along with a cup of orange juice, 2 cinnamon sticks, 10 cloves, ¼ cup sugar, and ¼ teaspoon nutmeg. Don't let it boil.

QUICK n' PAINLESS

Putting store-bought food in a pretty bowl or on a platter with garnish gives it a whole new life. Read the presentation section at the end of this chapter to make plain and simple look pretty fancy.

Cheese Ball and Crackers: I've made cheese balls and I've bought cheese balls; the bought ones are practically indistinguishable from the homemade kind, and they're sometimes even better. A cheese ball is one of those silly dishes that we laugh at and then fight for the knife to spread it on crackers. If you don't want round cheese on your table, though, serve several wedges of cheese on a wood board with a knife and selection of crackers.

Hot Spinach Dip with Tortilla Chips or Rye Bread: A hot dip makes the whole event feel more like a meal, especially when it's served with rye bread, although tortilla chips are good, too. This recipe is full of fat, but it's delicious, fragrant, and easy (and hey—it is the holidays!). Sauté one pound of spicy sausage meat with 1 chopped onion and 2 cloves of garlic that have been minced. Stir in two 10-ounce packages of frozen chopped spinach, one 8-ounce package of cream cheese, and 1 cup of store-bought salsa. Simmer for about 5 minutes until the spinach is cooked through. Serve it on a hot plate, if you like, or simply in a bowl—it stays hot for a while.

Store-bought Pastries, Cookies, Cakes: The stores are full of baked goodies and sweets at this time of year—avail yourself of them to make a pastry, cookie, or cake tray.

IF YOU'RE SO
INCLINED

If you want to really splurge, boil up a generous quantity of fresh large shrimp in their shells. (Plunge into boiling water for 2 to 3 minutes and drain immediately.) Serve the shrimp on top of a huge platter of ice, and place a bowl of commercially prepared cocktail sauce in the center of the platter. Make plenty—nobody ever gets enough shrimp at parties, so for Christmas, let them eat their fill!

Christmas Breakfast

A hearty Christmas breakfast before (or after!) opening gifts helps make the day more special and means you probably won't have to serve three meals, but only this big breakfast and your big dinner (whether afternoon or evening). The following menu is lavish and plentiful, but you actually get in and out of the kitchen quickly.

- Waffles with Orange Butter and Warm Syrup
- Bacon and Scrambled Eggs
- Sliced Fresh or Canned Pineapple
- Orange Juice and Coffee

Waffles with Orange Butter and Warm Syrup: Use frozen waffles, and bake them on a baking sheet instead of toasting them. Serve in a napkin-lined basket to keep them hot. The night before, mix 1 stick of softened butter with 1 tablespoon of orange zest and 1 tablespoon of orange juice. Don't refrigerate. Serve this orange butter with regular syrup; for an extra nice touch, put the syrup in a microwaveable pitcher and nuke it for less than a minute.

Bacon and Scrambled Eggs: Cook the bacon in the microwave while you beat the eggs. Cook scrambled eggs in a large skillet and pour them into a serving dish while they're still very wet. Serve immediately.

QUICK ⬤ PAINLESS

If your family is too eager to open gifts to even consider sitting down to breakfast, buy a large Danish ring, fruit stollen, saffron buns, or another sort of holiday pastry, and serve with coffee or hot chocolate around the tree.

Sliced Fresh or Canned Pineapple: Some fresh fruit finishes a leisurely holiday breakfast, but don't spend time slicing and dicing for fruit salad. If you can find a pineapple, slice off the outside, cut it in half lengthwise, cut it into quarters, and slice out the core. Cube and serve—or serve chunks (canned without syrup).

Orange Juice and Coffee: Leave coffee hot in the coffee maker, and pour orange juice directly from the carton into glasses instead of using a decorative glass pitcher.

QUICK n' PAINLESS

If you can't wait to open presents, but you also can't wait to eat, eat your Christmas breakfast picnic-style around the tree, on festive holiday paper plates. Clean-up is a breeze—just throw the plates out with the torn-up wrapping paper!

KIDS' BIRTHDAY PARTY

This is an easy one: You can spend all day cooking for a dozen kids, and they will smear whatever you make on their faces and on the carpet. Kids don't care about homemade—they want something they think is fun, so if you're having a party at home, order in several boxes of pizza.

- Pizza and Soft Drinks
- Carrot and Celery Sticks with Ranch Dip
- Birthday Cake and Ice Cream

Pizza and Soft Drinks: Children tend to like their pizza without a lot of stuff on it, so order plenty of plain cheese pizza. Serve the soda in plastic cups and use brightly colored paper party plates so that all the detritus goes directly into the garbage. If you're letting them build their own pizzas at home, buy the ready-made crusts in plastic bags or use pitas or even English muffins. Buy jars of pizza sauce, pregrated cheese, and presliced pepperoni.

Carrot and Celery Sticks with Ranch Dip: Of course you want to provide some vitamins and minerals for the little tykes. If you want to cut down your peeling and chopping time, buy bags of baby carrots. Place carrot and celery sticks on a plate alongside a bowl of store-bought Ranch dressing.

Congratulations! You had a children's birthday party where the host wasn't so exhausted that everyone went home crying! Put your little birthday boy or girl down for a nap and treat yourself to a nice soak in the bathtub.

The Lazy Way

Birthday Cake and Ice Cream: It's obligatory to serve birthday cake and ice cream, but you don't have to make the cake yourself. Buy a cake and a half gallon of ice cream, and don't forget the candles.

QUICK n' PAINLESS

As an alternative, make the food part of the party entertainment. Set out pizza crusts (ready-made and baked from the supermarket) and toppings and let kids build their own pies. This should keep them so busy that they won't even notice the absence of the clown!

COCKTAIL PARTY

If you entertain grownups, there's a wealth of elegant finger foods that don't require you to stand in the kitchen, piping fillings into baked shells. Go with dips and spreads so that your guests do the dipping and spreading themselves. A sample menu follows, but check out Chapter 7, "Quick-to-Make Quick Bites," for more ideas. Serving all wine or all champagne is not only cheaper than stocking a full bar but much, much easier. Be sure to have some sparkling water and soft drinks on hand as well, and then simply smile and ask, "Red or white?"

- Olives
- Goat Cheese and Crackers
- Pâté and French Bread
- Store-bought Cheese Straws
- Crudites and Bleu Cheese Dip

Olives: Buy a selection of olives at a gourmet store, and serve them with small bowls nearby where pits can be discreetly stored. Marinated, flavored olives are ideal.

Goat Cheese and Crackers: Try the Goat Cheese with Pesto recipe on page 94, or serve the cheese plain. You can also buy delicious flavored goat cheeses rolled in herbs or crushed pepper.

Pâté and French Bread: Tear, don't slice, crusty baguettes into small chunks, and pile them in a basket next to a spreadable, room-temperature pâté.

YOU'LL THANK YOURSELF LATER

Less is more: Don't commit yourself to making a heap of things—too many items are not as memorable as a few great dishes.

Store-bought Cheese Straws: Cheese Straws take a lot of time to make, what with mixing the dough and rolling or piping them onto a baking sheet, but they can also be found in the cracker section of the supermarket. They're tasty, they're retro, and nothing is better with a drink than a spicy and salty little nibble.

Crudites and Bleu Cheese Dip: A platter of cut-up fresh vegetables requires the most effort on your part, but it's almost required that you have something besides the salty stuff. Don't spend a lot of time thinly slicing peppers and peeling carrots, when you can just break up cauliflower and broccoli into florets, or serve finger-ready snow peas. Celery is also fast and easy to slice and doesn't require peeling (see "Lookin' Good: Sprucing Up Store-Bought Dishes and Presenting Home-Cooked Food," page 285). Serve veggies alongside a bowl of store-bought bleu cheese dip.

YOU'LL THANK YOURSELF LATER

Evaluate your strengths. Do people adore your hot spinach dip and ignore your eggplant caviar? Are you famous for the strudel you make once every two years? Put your efforts into the memorable dishes and buy—or strike from the menu— the less exciting ones. Most cooks have too much food for large family events rather than too little.

THANKSGIVING

It's hard to imagine Thanksgiving with a pared-down menu, but this is about as stripped-down a version as most people would dare to serve to families and friends who expect a huge feast. This is not a gourmet Thanksgiving, but it's delicious, satisfying, and simple to assemble. Substitute and supplement according to your family traditions, but give yourself permission to take it easy.

Having the ham or turkey cooked by a hand other than your own might sound like a holiday sacrilege, but it's fast, relatively inexpensive, and, unless you're really an acknowledged turkey expert, it usually results in a tastier product.

There are some terrific national brands of ready-made, unbaked pumpkin pie, and you can bake them yourself to let that spicy smell drift out from the kitchen. You probably can't hide the fact that it's a store-bought pie, but cover it with enough whipped cream and nobody cares!

- Turkey, Stuffing, and Gravy
- Cranberry Sauce
- Mashed Potatoes
- Sweet Potatoes
- Green Beans
- Cold Salad Platter
- Dinner Rolls
- Pumpkin Pie and Whipped Cream

YOU'LL THANK YOURSELF LATER

Use the freezer. If you know far in advance that you're hosting Thanksgiving this year, whip up that famous pie of yours on a rainy fall day when the kids are at friends. For a big meal like this, making lists and planning to do some things in advance will make the holiday far more stress-free.

Turkey, Stuffing, and Gravy: The biggest part of the labor—turkey, stuffing, and gravy—can all be purchased from a deli or caterer. Because it's a special occasion, take the time before you order a pre-roasted turkey to check around and make sure you get a reliable one. Most supermarket delis that roast turkeys have a sample that you can taste, as do some caterers and food shops. Most places that roast the holiday bird also supply all the trimmings, from mashed potatoes to rolls, but it's nice to cook some of it yourself, to make the house smell of food and to make sure there's a generous plenty of everything. It's usually a good idea to buy your stuffing and gravy from the same supplier unless you have a special stuffing that you always make and that everyone expects. If your homemade stuffing is part of the occasion, get the turkey and gravy from the same place and bake your stuffing by itself in a pan. When you open the hot bird and start carving, the house will smell of turkey, just as it should.

Cranberry Sauce: Buy canned cranberry sauce, whole or jellied. If nobody eats it, year after year, just leave it off your menu altogether—but there's usually some purist who'll say, "Hey! Where's the cranberry sauce?"

Mashed Potatoes: Mashed potatoes are usually considered a given and it's hard to get around making them. To avoid spending hours at the sink amid all the hustle of a holiday morning, peel the potatoes the night before and leave them sitting in cold water overnight (water must cover them completely). About an hour before you plan

IF YOU'RE SO
INCLINED

I make an uncooked cranberry relish that I find far more delicious than the cooked and canned kind. Place 1 bag of washed fresh cranberries in the food processor with one quartered orange (skin and all), and add 3/4 cup sugar. Process until finely ground, but not pureed. Store refrigerated until ready to use. It is excellent on turkey sandwiches the next day.

Whether you buy your Thanksgiving pie or bake one, buy or bake double, and store the extra in the freezer for Christmas. It's less than a month away, and that's one dessert out of the way for the next holiday.

to eat, cook, drain, and mash with butter and milk. Leave them sitting on the back of the stove, covered, with a layer of hot milk over the top to be stirred in before serving.

Sweet Potatoes: Not everyone likes sweet potatoes, but they usually make an appearance on the Thanksgiving table. For ease, buy them canned, not fresh, and bake them at 350° for half an hour with a sprinkle of brown sugar and orange zest (add mini-marshmallows, if you like).

Green Beans: Serve canned or frozen green beans, corn, or another vegetable on the side, with some butter stirred in for added flavor.

Cold Salad Platter: Because green salad doesn't always work well with gravy-covered Thanksgiving food, lay out a dish with cold pickles (try pickled onions, beets, and peppers for a change) and crudites for guests to poke around the edges of their piled plates.

Dinner Rolls: This is not the day to be baking bread. If no one is bringing bread, buy bakery rolls that taste good without being heated.

Pumpkin Pie and Whipped Cream: Pumpkin pie is the easiest thing to ask a guest to bring. You can also buy good pies, either ready to serve or ready to be baked. Serve with plenty of whipped cream or ice cream and don't worry—most people are too full to eat dessert anyway.

LOOKIN' GOOD: SPRUCING UP STORE-BOUGHT DISHES AND PRESENTING HOME-COOKED FOOD

Serving and Presentation

- Always remove store-bought foods from their disposable containers and serve them on your own dishes, unless the food is a pie or some such item that would be damaged by lifting it out.

- Crudites don't have to be arranged in a circle around a platter with dip in middle. If all your trimmed veggies are long and tall (such as carrots, celery, and pepper strips), set them upright in thin drinking glasses, which you can place close together in a basket along with the bowl of dip.

- Meats and poultry may make a more stunning presentation on the platter when they're whole, but it's much more practical to serve them sliced. Arrange slices of meat in an overlapping pattern, divide poultry platters loosely into sections: breast slices overlapping at the front, dark meat piled to one side, wings or legs whole at the back.

- Dishes cooked in a casserole make a good presentation, especially when they have their own trivets, such as a whole browned tray of scalloped potatoes set into a purpose-made wicker basket, or a glass pan of sugar-topped sweet potatoes that fits into a sterling silver holder.

QUICK ⬛ PAINLESS

If you can't remove certain store-bought items from their containers, and you'd like to mask the foil pie dish or plastic tart tray, simply tie a pretty linen napkin, dish towel, bandanna, even dress scarf (as long as it's washable) around the container.

IF YOU'RE SO
INCLINED

If you really want to impress your guests, you can make "roses" out of certain vegetables like carrots, tomatoes, and of course, radishes. To make a carrot rose, peel lengthwise strips, using a vegetable peeler, from long, straight carrots. Curl each carrot strip around your forefinger and fasten the loose end with a toothpick. Place curl in a bowl of ice water and refrigerate for about 1 hour. Drain and remove toothpick. The cold water forces the carrot to keep the "rose" shape.

■ Don't serve dry starches such as bread and crackers flat on a plate, especially hot bread, which can become soggy where it touches the plate. Drape a linen napkin in a serving basket and heap the bread, rolls, toasts, or crackers in it.

■ Serve beautifully decorated cakes and tarts whole on decorative platters (even if they're still sitting on a cardboard base from the bakery).

■ Homey cakes such as pound cake and banana bread can be sliced and served still in their original shape on a platter, or lying overlapped in a curve or circle.

Garnishes and Additions

■ Garnish platters of chopped meats and poultry with sprigs of fresh parsley or rosemary.

■ Add chestnuts, walnuts, chopped apples, prunes, or raisins to store-bought stuffing.

■ Cover the faces of store-bought pies with whipped cream and a heavy sprinkle of chopped nuts where appropriate.

■ Nuts are a good garnish for savory foods as well: scatter chopped walnuts over pâté or soft cheese.

■ Add fresh parsley to a store-bought dip, from French onion dip to clam dip to hummus. Sprinkle cayenne or paprika over the top.

■ Put spices or herbs in store-bought sauces or toppings, such as fresh basil in spaghetti sauce or chopped fresh cilantro in salsa.

- Use edible flowers, available at some gourmet markets, to enliven green salads, float on soups, or decorate cakes.

- Surround cakes, pies, and tarts with fruits or whipped cream when appropriate, or lay a few sprigs of fresh mint around the platter.

- Lay cookies or cake slices on a platter with a pile of whole fruit that's both decorative and edible: a bunch of grapes, red apples, some fresh figs, even a handful of walnuts.

Decorations

Sometimes the most simple and natural items make the most beautiful decorations. You don't have to have taken a course in flower arranging to create a lovely centerpiece—a single, brightly colored gerber daisy or delicate white rose placed in a glass bud vase can create quite an effect. Or fill a pretty bowl with fruit; lemons piled in a glass dish always make a vibrant and refreshing display. So think natural!

- Candles are the busy entertainer's best friend. Use them all over the house (I even put a small one in the bathroom.) Not only do they hide the dust, but they really make a room much more lovely and festive.

- Use natural seasonal decorations such as bunches of Indian corn at Halloween and Thanksgiving and sprigs of holly and pine at Christmas. Place a small Christmas wreath face in the center of the table and

QUICK ☞ PAINLESS

To jazz up the standard clear glass votives and white candles, pour a little cranberry juice into the votive before you pop in the candle. The soft, red glow adds a nice touch at any time of the year.

set a fat red candle in the center. Hang flags for the Fourth of July; set a bunch of spring flowers and a small basket of colored eggs on the table for Easter.

- Get out your good china and crystal for any and all festive occasions and let your table look beautiful with it. Use your china and enjoy it instead of letting it collect dust in a china cabinet.

- Use big cloth napkins for festive meals, either a no-iron poly-cotton blend, or a pile of linen or cotton napkins that you'll drop off at the laundry instead of washing and ironing yourself.

- Flowers don't have to be incredibly expensive blooms from a florist. Many huge supermarkets have a small florist section near the produce department. Buy bunches of roses and irises and set them around the house—but don't put them in the center of the dinner table where they block conversation.

QUICK ☜ PAINLESS

Don't worry if you don't have enough of the same linen napkins. A combination of different colors and patterns creates a lively and interesting table setting. You may want to avoid using drastically different fabrics, like a seersucker and a wool, but feel free to be a little daring when it comes to color scheme.

Getting Time on Your Side

	The Old Way	The Lazy Way
Baking fresh rolls for a dinner party	3 hours	0 hours
Preparing all the desserts for your Christmas Eve party	12 hours	30 minutes (most of that time is for making up your mind at the bakery!)
Making waffles for Christmas breakfast	45 minutes	5 minutes (frozen!)
Having a birthday party for your 5-year-old and 7 of his rowdy little friends	2 days	5 hours (and that's including wiping ice cream off the wall)
Preparing Thanksgiving dinner for 15	3 days	6 hours (and a few phone calls)
Time it takes to recover after having your whole family over for the holidays	364 days	about a week

Part 4

More Lazy Stuff

How to Get Someone Else to Do It

The most comprehensive way to get someone else to cook your meals all the time is to install a full-time cook in the kitchen. That way, you can order dinner every morning on your way out the door. Since that doesn't fall into the lifestyle of most of us, however, we have to look elsewhere for help with our cooking.

If you just can't face cooking one more night, and you're about to give up altogether, give yourself a break. Cook now and then, and get someone else to do it other times—and that doesn't necessarily mean someone who lives with you. A few suggestions follow for when you don't feel like applying heat to raw ingredients.

LOW-KEY CATERING AND BUYING FOOD IN

- Easily available takeout food is often finger food: buckets of fried chicken or chicken wings, pizza, or burgers and fries. Even though this makes dinner quick, it doesn't necessarily make it healthy or delicious. Save one night a week, maybe Friday or Saturday, for a high-fat, high-sodium meal such as pizza, and look for healthier alternatives during the week.

- You might consider buying a cooked chicken, such as a rotisserie chicken, and then making your own accompaniments: stuffing mix and a green salad, or baked potatoes and steamed broccoli. Rice and green beans are also quick and easy, and if you're feeling extra adventurous, you can pop a pan of quick cornbread into the oven.

- Look for packaged frozen entrees, such as lasagna or beef stew, that can be served with your own bread and salad. Having your own side dishes with a precooked entree makes the meal practically indistinguishable from those you actually cooked yourself.

- Although there are many frozen versions of entrees, made by major national companies, that are quite good, sometimes the portions are often too skimpy to feed the family of four that the box says the contents will feed. Make two boxes if you need to so that "frozen lasagna night" doesn't leave your teenage son feeling starved and deprived.

- Find a tasty entree made by a small catering or food company in your area. You order their chicken stew with white wine and rosemary in the morning, and pick it up on the way home. Look in the phone book—a lot of towns and cities have small-scale food shops with names like "Complete Feasts" and "The Pantry."

- Call around to small catering companies or gourmet stores and see if the price you'd pay for a chicken pot pie or tub of fresh spaghetti sauce is worth your while. Even if you're paying $15 to $20 for a meal you could have made yourself for $5, it might be worth it to you in terms of time saved and food quality. Stock up on reasonably priced entrees that your family likes and store them in the freezer for busy nights.

- Shop at the fine deli and gourmet counters of upscale supermarkets. Many of these will make entrees as good as restaurant food, and give you a choice of healthy dishes as well as richer ones. If you can pick up items like a loaf of sourdough and four grilled chicken breasts, a tub of couscous and some asparagus in vinaigrette on the side, you may even stop cooking on weeknights!

- Sometimes, otherwise average supermarkets have surprisingly tasty food in their deli sections—and sometimes they don't. If it smells good, check it out. Some slices of roast ham, a tub of potato salad, a can of green beans, and you're set.

- More and more, supermarket delis are striving to improve their food. Tell them what you'd like to see—you may be surprised how responsive they are.

MAKING A GROUP EFFORT

- If you have a couple of close friends who have the same busy weekday situation that you do (such as soccer moms who also work), you might consider a round-robin style of preparing dinner with them.

- When you make a pan of lasagna or a chicken pie, make another one for each friend. When your friends make a ham and rice casserole or a pot of chili, you get a panful or a tubful. Each family prepares its own simple side dish, such as a green salad or a package of frozen vegetables.

- It's best not to try this with more than three cooks or the size of the meals you must prepare when it's your night to cook may be too big for your kitchen capacity. You don't have to eat each other's food every night—you can store her chicken pie in the fridge or freezer, and have pizza one night instead. This method should even out over time, however, so that with three cooks (and one night of takeout), you only have to cook dinner twice a week.

- This system tends to work best for people who have similar schedules and family sizes, and whose children are pursuing the same after school sports or who live in your neighborhood.

- Modify the system and make it suit your schedule and needs. Maybe you and one friend cooking double once a week is just enough to ease your kitchen burden. Maybe you have three close friends who can make it work. Maybe you and your sister-in-law can take turns feeding each other's kids a couple of times a week, giving each set of grown-ups a night to dine alone.

If You Really Want More, Read These

Getting food on the table the lazy way is all about simple and speedy cooking. A spate of quick-cooking cookbooks has hit the market in recent years, offering quick recipes ranging from the ultra kid-friendly (add some brown sugar and ketchup to a can of baked beans), to healthy (stir-fried turkey with snow peas and carrots), to haute cuisine entertaining (fillet of beef with wild mushrooms and truffles), to cooking by the seat of your pants (perfectly illustrated by Arthur Schwartz's terrific book *What to Cook When You Think There's Nothing in the House to Eat*). You should also be sure to check out the recipes for quick meals that can be found in many magazines, from *Ladies Home Journal* and *Women's Day* to *Bon Appetit,* which has the regular features devoted to quick cooking, "30-Minute Main Courses" and "Too Busy to Cook."

Anything you can't find or order in your local bookstore may be available on-line from an Internet bookseller. Here are a few of my favorite quick cooking books:

Cooking with Three Ingredients: Flavorful Food Easy as 1, 2, 3 by Andrew Schloss (HarperCollins, 1996).

The 15-Minute Chicken Gourmet by Paulette Mitchell (Macmillan, 1997).

Healthy Cooking for People Who Don't Have Time to Cook by Jeanne Jones (Rodale Press, 1997).

Simple Vegetarian Pleasures by Jeanne Lemlin (HarperCollins, 1998).

The 60-Minute Bread Book and Other Fast-Yeast Recipes You Can make in Half the Usual Time by Nancy Baggett (G.P. Putnam, 1985).

365 Easy One-Dish Meals by Natalie Haughton (HarperPerennial, 1990).

What to Cook When You Think There's Nothing in the House to Eat by Arthur Schwartz (HarperPerennial, 1992).

If You Don't Know What It Means, Look Here

Sure, you already knew that—but in case you don't immediately remember something while you're rushing through a quick-cooking recipe, here's a list of basic cooking terms.

Adjust: To correct the seasoning in a dish just before serving by adding more salt, pepper, herbs, spices, vinegar, etc.

Al dente: Italian for "to the tooth" and used to describe pasta cooked until it's still slightly firm and offers some resistance when you bite.

Baking Powder: A carefully balanced mixture of sodium bicarbonate and cream of tarter, which is used to leaven baked goods.

Baking Soda: Sodium bicarbonate; makes baked goods rise when used in conjunction with an acid such as buttermilk or baking soda. Also a terrific all-purpose household cleaner that can take the place of cleanser for most kitchen jobs.

Barbecue: To cook on an outdoor gas or charcoal grill.

Batter: A thin, liquid dough such as that made for pancakes, muffins, and cakes.

Beat: To mix at a high rate of speed in order to incorporate air into a dough or batter.

Blanch: A method by which vegetables or fruits (and sometimes nuts) are plunged into rapidly boiling water and then quickly rinsed in cold water. This makes broccoli and greens retain a bright color, and loosens the skins for easy peeling of tomatoes and peaches.

Blend: To combine ingredients with a smooth, gentle motion.

Boil: To raise a liquid to a high enough temperature that bubbles rise steadily to the surface.

Bread: *(verb)* To coat a food in fine crumbs (from bread, crackers, potato chips, ground nuts, etc.) to seal in moisture and form a crisp crust when fried.

Broil: To brown a food under a hot element, usually in the oven. Broiling achieves an attractively browned surface in a short amount of time with a minimum of fat.

Brown: To cook a food until the surface is colored. Browning occurs when surface sugars are heated until they turn a golden color.

Brush: *(verb)* To use a kitchen or pastry brush to coat food with a liquid, such as oil or milk. If you don't have a brush, you can use your fingers or a paper towel to dab oil on meats.

Bubble: Simmer; to let a food cook at an even heat just below a boil, with bubbles occasionally rising.

Chop: To cut a food into small pieces. Coarsely chopped is to cut into large, rough pieces without concern for evenness of size.

Core: To remove the inner part of a fruit or vegetable, such as cutting out the seeds of an apple.

Cream: *(verb)* To beat a mixture such as butter and sugar until it's smooth and lighter in color than when you began. *(noun)* The rich, butterfat rich liquid that rises to the surface of unhomogenized milk. Buy heavy cream for whipping. Half and half (part milk, part cream) or whole milk can be used for all recipes in this book that call for light cream.

Crumble: *(verb)* To break up a food, such as cheese or bread, usually with your fingers. *(noun)* A dessert of fruit baked with a sweet, crunchy topping.

Cube: To cut food into small, evenly sized squares.

Dash: A pinch; a small amount of a strong flavoring such as hot sauce or nutmeg that is added for a hint of flavor. A dash is usually about ⅛ teaspoon, but cooks add it by feel rather than measuring it, and by personal preference. One cook's dash of hot sauce may be 2 tablespoons to another's ¼ teaspoon.

Deglaze: To make a sauce incorporating the browned bits left in the bottom of a sauté pan by swirling wine or another liquid in the hot pan and then scraping it with a spatula.

Dice: To cut food into small, evenly sized cubes.

Dot: To cover the surface of a dish with bits of butter or cheese, etc., before baking or serving. Use a knife or your fingers to cut or crumble the material you're dotting into little bits as you work, scattering them over the surface.

Drain: To remove the liquid from a food, such as pouring pasta and its boiling water through a colander, or to remove liquid from canned or fresh foods by pouring it through a strainer. To drain canned food, hold the opened lid over the can and let the juice pour out around it, holding the food in with the lid.

Dredge: To coat a moist food in flour, cornmeal, bread crumbs, etc.

Drizzle: To pour a small amount of liquid over the surface of a food, such as pouring a little olive oil over the top of chicken pieces before baking them, or dripping a liquid icing over the surface of a cake, or sprinkling some balsamic vinegar over a platter of sliced tomatoes.

Dust: To sprinkle a dry ingredient over a dish, such a sifting a little powdered sugar over a cake, or sprinkling pepper on vegetables, or putting flour or cornmeal, etc. on raw food before cooking.

Fillet: *(noun)* A boneless piece of meat; *(verb)* to cut the bone out of a piece of meat to make a fillet.

Fold: To gently incorporate one ingredient into a mixture, such as folding egg whites into a batter.

Fry: To cook a food in oil at a high temperature. Deep frying is to totally submerge the food in oil.

Garnish: A last touch to a dish, for the sake of appearance as much as flavor, such as adding a few bright sprigs of parsley to a platter of cooked meat, or dusting Parmesan cheese over pasta just before serving.

Grate: To reduce foods such as cheese or carrots to fine strands by running them over a metal grater, either manually or with a food processor.

Grill: To cook over hot coals in an outdoor gas or charcoal brazier, or (usu. British) to cook meats or vegetables close up under a broiler.

Joint: To separate chicken or other meats into pieces along the natural joints, i.e. legs, wings.

Julienne: To chop food into fine matchsticks, both for appearance and quick cooking.

Marinate: To soak a food for a short time (15 minutes) or a long time (overnight) in a liquid that usually contains an acid, an oil, and a flavoring (such as lemon juice, olive oil, and oregano).

Mash: To smash a food, such as potatoes or turnips, into a smooth puree, either manually with a metal masher or by using electric beaters.

Mince: To chop a food into a very fine dice. When garlic is to be minced, it can always be pressed (see below) instead. (See also *press.*)

Pare: To peel a fruit or vegetable.

Poach: To cook a food such as eggs, fruit, or meat in a liquid until tender.

Pound: To flatten a food, such as chicken breasts, with a meat mallet or the palm of your hand to make it of even thickness for better cooking.

Preheat: To bring an oven fully to the required temperature before placing food in it.

Press (Garlic): To force a clove of garlic through a tool designed to push finely crushed garlic through a screen; using a garlic press is much faster than mincing it with a knife.

Puree: *(verb)* To reduce or grind a food to a fine, creamy consistency. Vegetable soups can be pureed in a blender or food processor, or in their pots with a hand-held immersion blender. *(noun)* A food that has been reduced to such a consistency.

Reduce: To simmer a food until much of its liquid is evaporated, thereby concentrating and intensifying flavors while thickening the consistency.

Roast: To cook a food uncovered in the oven until the exterior is well-browned.

Sauté: To quickly cook a food at a relatively high temperature in a small amount of oil.

Season: To add enough salt, pepper, herbs, or flavorings to a dish, usually just before serving.

Shred: To finely chop or grate a food into thin, small pieces.

Simmer: To keep a food just below boiling at an even heat, with a few bubbles rising now and then.

Steam: 1) To cook in a small amount of boiling water in a tightly covered pan. 2) To cook food over very hot water so that the steam does the cooking (and food doesn't have contact with the water).

Stew: Long, slow cooking in a small amount of liquid to produce a dish like a very thick soup. Tough meats are softened by stewing, and vegetables melt down to become deliciously tender.

Stir-Fry: A Chinese method of quickly cooking foods in a wok, at a very high temperature in a small amount of oil. Ingredients are all prepared in advance before stir-frying, and vegetables and meat are usually cut into small strips or pieces.

Stock: The flavorful liquid produced by slowly cooking meats or vegetables in water; used by gourmets for sauces, stews, gravies, etc. Stock is a wonderful addition to most foods, but the Lazy Kitchen prefers a stock cube, which can be reconstituted with hot water.

Strain: To separate solids from liquids with a sieve or colander.

Toss: To roughly mix ingredients such as salad and dressing or pasta and vegetables, using your hands or a fork and spoon.

Whip: To incorporate air into a food by beating vigorously with a spoon, fork, whisk, or beaters.

Whisk: *(verb)* To rapidly beat food in order to smooth it and/or to incorporate air. *(noun)* A balloon whisk is a metal tool that consists of several strands of looped stainless steel used to whip air into foods such as egg whites and cream.

Zest: *(noun)* The potent, fragrant, oil-filled outer rind of citrus fruits, used to flavor sweet and savory food. *(verb)* To remove the zest from a citrus fruit. When zesting, be sure to only peel off the very outer, colored layer of rind, and avoid the white pith below.

It's Time for Your Reward

Once You've Done This:
Stocked up your pantry

Reward Yourself:
Spend a little extra to buy some really top-quality ingredients, such as basmati rice imported from India.

Bought a food processor and figured out which other time-saving gadgets you will really use

Buy a coffee maker with a timer so you can wake up to the smell of fresh coffee.

Found space on the counter to store every piece of equipment that you'll use frequently and put the rest away on a high shelf

Bake a batch of cookies to try out your newly reorganized kitchen.

Finished cooking your first dinner according to *The Lazy Way*

Put on some music and let your family, friends, or significant other help clean up the kitchen.

Cooked meals *The Lazy Way* Monday through Thursday

Order in pizza on Friday night and eat off paper plates.

Baked muffins on a leisurely Sunday morning

Eat some of them warm and store the rest tightly sealed in foil. Heat in the microwave for a few seconds to catch that cozy, home-baked feeling on a weekday morning.

Once You've Done This:	**Reward Yourself:**
Remembered to make and freeze a double batch of caramelized onions (page 101)	Make a quick bowl of French Onion Soup with extra cheese to eat in front of a fire on a cold night with your loved one.
Cooked and eaten fish at least two nights a week	Have a special healthy dessert, such as a whole bowl of fresh raspberries.
Made at least three Lazy one-pot suppers	Celebrate with a special night of super-easy Lazy Lasagna (page 190), red candles, and a nice bottle of Chianti.
Added a whole lot more vegetables to your diet with the recipes for Lazy salads	Take a brisk walk around the block and maybe stop for a small ice cream—after all, you're eating tons more fiber now!
Hosted a Lazy Birthday Party	Put your little birthday boy or girl down for a nap (you can do this even if the party was for your husband), and take a long hot soak in a bath with lots of bubbles.
Cut some of those ties that bind and celebrated a Lazy Thanksgiving by buying some food and letting others bring plenty of the rest	Open a few bottles of Champagne and really enjoy a family holiday for a change.

Swaps and Substitutions

Before we were married, my future husband had grave reservations about me when he sent me to the store for chicken stock cubes while he cooked a special dinner, and I, unable to find any, returned with a package of instant cream of chicken soup.

Perfectionists and people who have a lot of time to cook can't understand how busy cooks like us can make such radical substitutions; they'd rather not make something at all than use the "wrong" ingredients. But cooking rules are made to be broken, and, although you may end up with an entirely different dish...well, if it tastes good, who cares? Don't be afraid to use whatever you have on hand in order to move ahead with your recipe.

And I must admit that my husband was right about the instant cream of chicken soup—as an older and wiser cook, I now know that I should have bought a package of instant chicken noodle and strained the noodles out!

If You Don't Have...	You Can Use...
Buttermilk	Yogurt
Sour cream	Plain yogurt OR 1 cup milk plus 2 tablespoons white vinegar or lemon juice (leave for 10 minutes)

If You Don't Have...	You Can Use...
Cream (for cooking only)	1/2 cup milk plus 1/4 cup melted butter
Self-rising flour	1 cup all-purpose flour plus 1 1/2 teaspoons baking powder plus 1/8 teaspoon salt
Baking powder	1 part baking soda to 2 parts cream of tartar
Eggs (for a cake only)	1/2 teaspoon baking soda plus 1 tablespoon vinegar, added to cake batter just before pouring into pans and baking (this will replace 2 eggs)
Sugar	Light corn syrup
Light Corn Syrup	Honey
Brown Sugar	White sugar and molasses
Confectioner's Sugar	Granulated sugar, finely ground in blender or food processor
Unsweetened Chocolate	3 tablespoons cocoa plus 1 tablespoon cooking oil
Semisweet Chocolate	3 tablespoons cocoa plus 1 tablespoon cooking oil plus 3 tablespoons sugar
Wine (for cooking only)	Apple juice with wine vinegar added, sherry, or vermouth
Tomato paste	Ketchup or sieved canned tomatoes

If You Don't Have...	You Can Use...
Worcestershire sauce	Splash of A1 steak sauce
Dijon mustard	Yellow mustard, a pinch of sugar, and a splash of white wine vinegar
Fresh chilis	Red chili flakes
Fresh ginger	Ground ginger
Bread crumbs	Crushed corn flakes or crackers
Wide egg noodles	Fettucinne
Rice	Mashed potatoes
Pork	Beef
Turkey	Chicken

Where to Find What You're Looking For

Now you can do these tasks, too!

Starting to think there are a few more of life's little tasks that you've been putting off? Don't worry—we've got you covered. Take a look at all of *The Lazy Way* books available. Just imagine—you can do almost anything *The Lazy Way!*

Clean Your House The Lazy Way
By Barbara H. Durham
0-02-862649-4

Handle Your Money The Lazy Way
By Sarah Young Fisher and Carol Turkington
0-02-862632-X

Care for Your Home The Lazy Way
By Terry Meany
0-02-862646-X

Train Your Dog The Lazy Way
By Andrea Arden
0-87605180-8

Take Care of Your Car The Lazy Way
By Michael Kennedy and Carol Turkington
0-02-862647-8

Learn Spanish The Lazy Way
By Vivian Isaak and Bogumila Michalewicz
0-02-862650-8

*All Lazy Way books are just $12.95!

additional titles on the back!

Build Your Financial Future The Lazy Way

By Terry Meany

0-02-862648-6

Shed Some Pounds The Lazy Way

By Annette Cain and Becky Cortopassi-Carlson

0-02-862999-X

Organize Your Stuff The Lazy Way

By Toni Ahlgren

0-02-863000-9

Feed Your Kids Right The Lazy Way

By Virginia Van Vynckt

0-02-863001-7

Cut Your Spending The Lazy Way

By Leslie Haggin

0-02-863002-5

Stop Aging The Lazy Way

By Judy Myers, Ph.D.

0-02-862793-8

Get in Shape The Lazy Way

By Annette Cain

0-02-863010-6

Learn French The Lazy Way

By Christophe Desmaison

0-02-863011-4

Learn Italian The Lazy Way

By Gabrielle Euvino

0-02-863014-9

Keep Your Kids Busy The Lazy Way

By Barbara Nielsen and Patrick Wallace

0-02-863013-0